# RACIAL PREJUDICE IN IMPERIAL ROME

THE J. H. GRAY LECTURES FOR 1966

# RACIAL PREJUDICE IN IMPERIAL ROME

BY

## A. N. SHERWIN-WHITE

*Fellow of St John's College, Oxford*

CAMBRIDGE
AT THE UNIVERSITY PRESS
1967

Published by the Syndics of the Cambridge University Press
Bentley House, 200 Euston Road, London N.W.1
American Branch: 32 East 57th Street, New York, N.Y. 10022

© Cambridge University Press 1967

Library of Congress Catalogue Card Number: 67–14287

Printed in Great Britain
by The Whitefriars Press Ltd., London and Tonbridge

# CONTENTS

# PREFACE

These lectures were given to the Faculty of Classical Literature and Archaeology in Cambridge University on the welcome invitation of the Gray Trustees as the Gray Memorial lectures for 1965–6. They were delivered to an agreeably large audience of dons and undergraduates, and I had the latter particularly in mind as I wrote. Hence while the lectures were intended as a contribution to learning I avoided an excess of erudition. They have been printed much as delivered, with the addition only of source references, a skeletal bibliography, and translations of most quotations, for the benefit of any wider audience, in the belief that a job is only made worse by patching and tinkering.

I chose this subject from among my interests because it has in the past received very unequal treatment. Little serious attention has been given to Roman *opinion* about the northern barbarians, and more study has been devoted to what the Greeks thought of their Roman masters than to the converse; even the antisemitism of the empire has generally been examined from the particular angles of Alexandrian politics or of the history of the early Church. I have concentrated on those parts of the evidence that offer most coherence in time and space—the Roman attitude to the northern barbarians from Caesar to Tacitus, the Jewish question in much the same period from about 50 B.C. to A.D. 100, and the *Graeculus* theme illustrated most expressly by Pliny, Tacitus, Juvenal and Lucian in the second century A.D. Inevitably I have left much undiscussed; three lectures gave me no time for Philo, Plutarch or Dio of Prusa. But others are at work in those fields, and in the meantime I offer these three lectures as a propaedeutic to a subject of great contemporary interest that has not, I believe, yet received a general survey.

It is my pleasant duty to record my warm thanks to the Gray Trustees for the opportunity of lecturing in Cambridge, and to the Faculty for the bounteous hospitality and patient attention which made my visit a most rewarding occasion.

OXFORD

*December 1966*

A. N. S-W.

# 1

# THE NORTHERN BARBARIANS IN STRABO AND CAESAR

## *Strabo and the Northerners*

It is a commonplace to assert that the ancient world knew nothing of colour bar and racial prejudice, and to illustrate this thesis by pointing out the assimilation of foreigners and barbarians into the culture of the Roman empire or the Hellenism of the Greek kingdoms. The assertion is worth probing. At the same superficial level one could counter with Graeco-Roman contempt for barbarians, Greek gibes against particular races, such as Carians and Lydians, Roman sneers at trousered Gauls and their fears of ferocious Germans, and Roman contempt for the Greeks themselves, while round the corner lurks the factor of antisemitism in the ancient world. If there was no racial prejudice, there certainly was some culture prejudice. The question is, how much, how deep, and whether or why it became a problem in the Roman empire.

The first necessity is to look again at the Graeco-Roman accounts of alien peoples and to question the witnesses.[1] What did they admire, and what did they distrust in foreign peoples? Strabo is the fullest witness, who has a great deal to say about the barbarism of foreign peoples, and particularly

[1] The theme of these lectures seems largely to have eluded modern discussions of the writings of Caesar. Neither E. A. Thompson, *The Early Germans* (Oxford, 1965), nor M. Rambaud, *La... Déformation Historique chez César*[2] (Paris, 1966), nor even J. H. Collins, *Propaganda, ethics and psychological assumptions in Caesar's writings* (Diss. Frankfort a.M., 1952) concern themselves with these topics. Nor does J. Jüthner's *Hellenen und Barbaren* (Leipzig, 1923) deal with Strabo at all.

of the Iberians, Celts and Germans of Spain and northern Europe. Of these, the Romans succeeded in assimilating the first two into the Latin civilization, while mostly failing with the latter. Strabo bestrode three worlds, writing in the times of Augustus as the Hellenistic recorder of the barbarian provinces of Rome. Here I may remark in parenthesis that it does not matter for present purposes how much Strabo has taken from the earlier geography of Posidonius, and how much he has observed or collected on his own account.[1] It is the selection that matters, and the use that he makes of the stuff. Without seeking to distinguish the layers of Strabo's material, it may suffice to note that his account of the Romanization and spread of Latin rights and customs in southern Spain and Gaul is certainly Strabo's own contribution. The description of the Turdetani and Volcae as people of the toga could not have been made till after the dictatorship of Julius Caesar, who was mainly responsible for the extensive grants of Roman privileges in these regions. As for the Germanic peoples, Strabo himself comments on the great extension of knowledge effected by the wars of Augustus.[2] So I am content to take Strabo to be speaking with his own tongue and often with his own mind and from his own observations. What then are the criteria that Strabo applies to barbarian peoples, what does he single out to distinguish them for praise or blame?

There is an illuminating contrast in Strabo's account of the southern Spaniards and of the mountain peoples of

[1] On this see J. Morr, ' Die Quellen von Strabons drittem Buch ', *Philologus* Suppl. 18.3 (1926), and W. Aly, *Strabonis Geographica* IV (Bonn, 1957), 109 f., 114 f., 304 f. Posidonius is not the sole source of Strabo's facts and opinions, though he bulks large.

[2] Strabo 7.1.4 (291), 2.4 (294). For Caesar's grants in Spain see M. I. Henderson, *JRS* 1942, 1 ff.

Lusitania and Tarraconensis. The Turdetani of Baetica, he says, are the cleverest of the Iberians.[1] They have a literature of their own—γραμματική is his word—prose and verse of what he calls ' the ancient tradition ', and six thousand lines of native laws written in metre. He asserts of no other barbarian people in Europe that it had a written literature, not even of the Celtic bards. He connects this fact with the agricultural wealth of Baetica, the land of the Turdetani, saying straight out that the consequence of its fertility was τὸ ἥμερον and τὸ πολιτικόν[2]—' civilized society '. By this he means civilization of urban or city-state type, as in other contexts. For he adds that the neighbours of the Turdetani had similar advantages but less so, because they lived in villages. This leads to a famous passage describing the final Romanization of the Turdetani and their neighbours. ' They have adopted the Roman style altogether, no longer remembering their own language, and become a people of the toga.' [3] He contrasts the happy condition of these peoples with their former style when they were the most bestial of all peoples. What he means by that emerges from his sketch of the Lusitanians, who were a strange folk in every way.[4] These have a simple diet—acorn meal is their main food. They drink water or beer instead of wine, use butter instead of olive oil, and they sleep on the ground, a custom that always seems to shock Strabo. They have long hair and black clothing, and they sleep in their clothes. Among peculiar customs they stone criminals and expose the sick. Worse still they maim prisoners of war, and practise divination by disembowelling

[1] *Ibid.* 3.1.6 (139).
[2] *Ibid.* 3.2.15 (151).
[3] *Ibid.*, summarized.
[4] *Ibid.* 3.3.6–8 (154–5), covering the northern mountain folk also.

3

them. The best that Strabo can say for the Lusitanians is that
they live in the Spartan style, and their marriage customs are
like the Hellenic. But taken altogether they are a wild people
—ἀγριωδής. This is due to their geographical isolation, which
leads to a lack of τὸ κοινωνικόν and τὸ φιλάνθρωπον—a sense
of community and common humanity.[1]

The same leading ideas appear in Strabo's account of the
Celtiberians. They were famous for having a thousand cities,
but these says Strabo were only villages—κῶμαι or hill-top
townships. The nature of their land was against the development of cities because of its roughness and its isolation—the
word is ἐκτοπισμόν—'the cultivated state'.[2] Hence they
lacked the quality of τὸ ἥμερόν. The Iberians in general
were much given to small raids and plundering expeditions.
But they did not combine in large operations, and so lacked
the achievement of greatness.[3] They, too, like the Lusitanians
have no vines or olives. Strabo attributes this not to soil or
climate but to human neglect—τὴν ὀλιγωρίαν τῶν ἀνθρώπων. It
is because they do not live πρὸς διαγωγήν[4] but in a scruffy
fashion, following the impulses and necessities of beasts.
Πρὸς διαγωγήν. This is a favourite term with Strabo. Literally
it means 'in an instructed fashion', or 'according to the
rule-book'. Strabo makes the point strongly, for he continues, 'It is not living πρὸς διαγωγήν to wash in ripe urine.'
He really was disgusted at the Iberians. They lack simplicity,
a quality which he approved in barbarians, notably in the
Celts of Gaul.[5] The women were even worse than the men.[6]
Strabo was very put off by their peculiar dress and still more
by their savagery—ὠμότης—an extreme word—and their

---

[1] *Ibid.* 8 (155).
[2] *Ibid.* 3.4.13 (163).
[3] *Ibid.* 3.4.5 (158).
[4] *Ibid.* 3.4.16 (164).
[5] *Ibid.* 3.4.5 (158).
[6] *Ibid.* 3.4.17 (164).

bestiality in desperate circumstances—ἀπόνοια θηριώδης. He instances their habit of slaying their children after defeat in war. This reminds him of a horrid story about the Cantabrian menfolk, who when crucified by the Romans sang at the stake.[1] He does not admire this—it horrifies him. He notes with less disapproval their marriage customs. These tended to matriarchy, which he says was not really civilized though not bestial, because matriarchy is not πανὺ πολιτικόν.[2] An interesting remark: ' It does not go with city government of the Hellenic sort.'

What one observes in all this is a very strong repugnance for the elements of savagery in these peoples, and an intolerant attitude towards mere differences in way of life such as food, clothing and domestic manners. People who sleep on the ground, drink water, and eat acorn bread are ' nasty '. People who live in villages, even if of an advanced culture, are less excellent than those who live in centralized cities. But Strabo does not regard these failings as due to the intrinsic nature of the barbarians. It is the result of material circumstances, ἐκτοπισμός, λυπρότης χώρας. It can and does change when the circumstances alter. The wildness of the Lusitanians has been reduced by the establishment of peace and by intercourse with the Romans.[3] Celtiberians, who were once the most bestial of all, have become wearers of togas.[4] The mountainfolk among the Artabrians were without laws because they had poor land. Lack of good land led to brigandage, and hence came inter-tribal wars and the destruction of agriculture, and hence the disappearance of law.[5] The underlying thought is that law and property go together, and

---

[1] *Ibid.* 3.4.18 (165).      [2] *Ibid.*, strictly, ' the rule of wives '.
[3] *Ibid.* 3.3.8 (156).      [4] *Ibid.* 3.2.15 (151), 4.20 (167).
[5] *Ibid.* 3.3.5 (154).

the standard is an approximation to the Greek or Roman way of life.

Strabo's critical differentia of race and civilization can be elucidated from his accounts of the peoples of Gaul, Germania and Britain, whom, apart from the Aquitanian tribes, he considered to be related and yet distinct. He begins in Book Four with a very revealing sentence. He says that the Aquitanians are distinct from Celts in language and body (σῶμα)—and are closer to the Iberians,[1] whereas the Celts and Belgae are alike in language and appearance—ὄψιν. The terms—ὄψιν, σῶμα—might indicate a purely physical and anthropometric distinction. But in a later passage he says that the Aquitanians differ from the Celts in σωμάτων κατασκεναί —the fashion of their bodies—and in language.[2] He is here thinking not only of physical attributes such as size, pigment and type of hair, but of the cultural characteristics to which he pays so much attention—style of clothing, head-dress, jewelry and ornaments. He stresses that the Celtic peoples wore cloaks and trousers and had long hair, and were fond of bangles and necklets of gold.[3]

Strabo's distinction between the Celts of Gaul and the Germanic folk is somewhat ambiguous. First he says that as the Celts are now under Roman rule and lack independence one must turn to the Germans to find out what the Celts are really like.[4] For Celts and Germans are akin, and alike in nature and social organization—πολιτεύματα. Later he says that the Germans are a little different from the Celts, being bigger, fiercer and fairer, but otherwise alike in shapes—

---

[1] *Ibid.* 4.1.1 (176). Cf. n. 1. p. 7.
[2] *Ibid.* 4.2.1 (189). Cf. 3.4.17 (164), where βαρβαρικὴ ἰδέα refers to ornaments.
[3] *Ibid.* 4.4.3 (196).     [4] *Ibid.* 4.4.2 (195–6).

μορφαί—characters and lives.[1] By shapes he evidently means, as by ὄψις earlier, features of dress and ornament. He draws attention to the custom of folk migration as common to both. When Strabo turns to the Britons, of whom he had himself seen specimens at Rome, he says that they were taller, thinner and less fair of hair than the Celts of Gaul, and that their customs were simpler and more barbaric.[2] He quotes as examples their ignorance of certain techniques. Though they have plenty of milk they make no cheese. They grow no garden crops, and their only townships according to his information are woodland places of refuge walled with thickset hedges.

Strabo would seem to make no distinction between peoples purely on physical grounds. He has three main criteria: physique, language and customs, but finds these difficult to apply. He makes a physical distinction between Celts and Germans, and between Britains and Germans, and a linguistic distinction between Aquitanians and Celts. But he finds a close similarity in customs and lives, including what he calls shapes, between Germans and Celts. It is remarkable that he mentions no linguistic difference between Gallic Celts and Germans, though Caesar knew that the language of Ariovistus was not the Celtic of eastern Gaul.[3] The great difference between Celts and Germans in Strabo is in their way of life, in the predominance among the Germans of stock-keeping and folk migration, and the relative absence of agriculture. The Germans dwell in huts and live off herds like nomads, whereas Gaul has become a land of tillers and plough-men.[4] But this was only a difference of degree. Strabo keeps returning to the point that the Celts of Gaul had given up the

---

[1] *Ibid.* 7.1.2 (290).

[2] *Ibid.* 4.5.2 (200).

[3] Caesar, *B.G.* I.47.4.

[4] Strabo 4.4.2 (196), 7.1.3–4 (291).

old warlike way of life on the Germanic pattern, and turned
to agriculture, as the result of the Roman conquest,[1] first of
Provence and later of northern Gaul.[2]

As in Spain so also in Gaul and Germany; the real barrier
between Greeks or Romans and barbarians lies in customs
and way of life. The Celts of northern Gaul, he says, *still*
sleep on the ground and eat their meals sitting on mattresses
of straw.[3] They eat meat and milk, live in wooden houses, and
inhabit villages—κῶμαι in Strabo's terminology.[4] There is a
characteristic passage about the Allobroges of the middle
Rhone and their chief place Vienna.[5] This had developed into
a real city. Formerly it was a κώμη—township—but now it
is the metropolis of the Allobroges, and all the noble families
live there. This is the great transformation, the act of grace,
in Strabo's eyes. It is the consequence of the Roman conquest,
and of the consolidation of agriculture as the primary
economic pattern. In a similar passage that may hearken back
two generations to Posidonius he remarks that all the barbarians around Massilia were turning to farming and the
practice of city life—πρὸς πολιτείας καὶ γεωργίας.[6] In a complementary passage from his description of the Germans he
attributes their migratory customs to the lack of agriculture
and the absence of the habit of storing up wealth.[7] He uses a
telling phrase: τὸ μὴ θησαυρίζειν.

Strabo's criterion for customs is not entirely materialist.
He recognizes distinctions of temperament and behaviour.

---

[1] *Ibid.* 4.1.11 (186), 14 (189). For Celtic stock-keeping see 4.4.3 (197)—
among Belgae.
[2] *Ibid.* 4.1.2 (178), 5 (180), 4.2 (195).
[3] *Ibid.* 4.4.3 (197). For beds cf. 3.3.7 (155).
[4] *Ibid.* 4.1.11 (186), 12 (186).
[5] *Ibid.* 4.1.11 (186).
[6] *Ibid.* 4.1.5 (180).
[7] *Ibid.* 7.1.3 (291)

The Celts are warlike, passionate and quick to take sides and fight for those who have suffered a wrong.[1] This temperament he defines as τὸ ἁπλοῦν καὶ οὐ κακόηθες, 'an honest simplicity'. This may be interpreted by what he said of the Iberians who had the opposite qualities: τὸ πανοῦργον φύσει καὶ τὸ μὴ ἁπλοῦν.[2] Evidently he regarded the Iberians as dour and malicious, and the Celts as direct and generous. Elsewhere he adds that the Celts of Gaul were boastful and ' light '—κοῦφοι. He means ' light ' in the sense of frivolous fondness for personal ornaments and also of being easily excited and depressed. For he says that this ' lightness ' made them violent in their reaction to defeat or victory.[3] Then he adds the comment that in addition to this lack of reasoned behaviour the northern peoples have a great deal of uncivilized wildness—τὸ ἔκφυλον, anti-social behaviour,[4] a term of strong condemnation in Strabo. In this passage he is trying to distinguish between human weaknesses of temperament that are common to all men, and something that he considers to be characteristically barbaric. What he has in mind turns out to be the savagery associated with the treatment of prisoners and sacrificial victims—the decapitation of enemies, the preservation of skulls as trophies, human sacrifice of various sorts, and forms of divination ' contrary to our customs '.[5]

Finally he gives a horrid account of the holy women on an island in the Loire who tear their victims limb from limb in what he regards as Bacchic rites.[6] In his description of the

---

[1] *Ibid.* 4.4.2 (195).
[2] *Ibid.* 3.4.5 (158).
[3] *Ibid.* 4.4.5 (197).
[4] Cf. the use of ἔκφυλος in Philo, *Index Verborum*, ed. J. Leisegang (Berlin, 1926), vii, i, 238.
[5] Strabo 4.3.5 (198).
[6] *Ibid.* 4.3.6 (198).

Germanic Cimbri he dilates upon the female seers who drain prisoners of their blood and use it for divination.[1] He had mentioned a practice of this sort among the Lusitanians of Spain,[2] but he dwells upon it most in his account of Gaul as a thing contrary to 'our custom', and remarks with approval that the Romans have put a stop to some of these dodges.[3]

It is remarkable that Strabo does not make religious practice a regular criterion of cultural difference. The explanation is to hand that he or Posidonius, if you like, found the religious similarities greater than the differences. He has very little to say about the religious *ideas* of the barbarians. His acceptance of the identification of the orgies on the island in the Loire as Bacchic is doubtless characteristic. He does go out of his way to remark that some say that the Gallaeci of north-west Spain were godless—ἄθεοι—but that the Celtiberians celebrated festivals at full moon to a nameless deity.[4] This context suggests that by ἄθεοι he meant what was intended a century later when the Christians were called ἄθεοι —that the religious ideology of the Callaeci bore no relation to that of the rest of the world at that time. What Strabo occasionally picks out as a differential is not the religious ideology of barbarians but their priestly organization, notably when discussing the Druids and seers of the Celts[5] and the female priests and prophets of the Germanic Cimbri.[6] The Druidic organization made a great impression on Greeks and Romans. Strabo, like Caesar, picks it out as exceptional. There was nothing comparable in Graeco-Roman experience to this secret society or brotherhood of aristocratic witch-

---

[1] *Ibid.* 7.2.3 (294).
[2] *Ibid.* 3.3.6 (154).
[3] *Ibid.* 4.4.5 (198).
[4] *Ibid.* 3.4.16 (164).
[5] *Ibid.* 4.4.4 (197).
[6] *Ibid.* 7.2.3 (294).

doctors, who had a traditional discipline concerned both with the management of the gods and with intellectual doctrines of a metaphysical sort. This powerful brotherhood, which had a hand in all major political issues, stood outside the ordinary Celtic system of elective tribal magistrates and priests, which in essence closely resembled the Graeco-Roman pattern. So the Druids appear in Strabo as the institution that marked out the peculiarity of the Celts. Strabo, unlike Caesar, does not specifically say that the Druids were limited to the Celts of Gaul and Britain, though his silence may imply what Caesar states—that the Germanic tribes did not have the Druidic system.[1]

Strabo is not only concerned with differentials. He looks, not always with great success, for resemblance or analogies between the barbarian and the Graeco-Roman civilization. He discovers moral philosophy among the Druids, and what he calls *grammatice* among the intelligent Turdetani.[2] Among the barbarians of Lusitania he found *agones*, or competitive festivals, of various sorts, and a Hellenic marriage rite.[3] But he had to admit that the division of labour between men and women in Celtic Gaul was 'different from ours, as is commonly the way with barbarian peoples'.[4] Oddly, he finds that the very savage Dardanians of Illyricum, a people of the Celtic fringe who lived in caves and dunghills, were nevertheless devoted to music of a kind.[5]

The great value of Strabo's account perhaps lies in this. He shows how strong was the sense of cultural superiority and cultural difference possessed by an educated Greek of the late Hellenistic world, how violent was the shudder of horror

---

[1] Caesar *B.G.* VI 21.1.    [2] Strabo 3.1.6 (139).
[3] *Ibid.* 3.3.7 (155).    [4] *Ibid.* 4.4.3 (197).
[5] *Ibid.* 7.5.7 (316).

that such a man felt at the savage ferocity of the remote barbarians, the peoples who lived in huts and caves, in its extreme manifestations. Yet he possessed an open mind. He is no romantic believer in innocent savages uncorrupted by civilization. He is fair when he finds some laudable characteristics, but on the whole he does not find much to admire in the temperament and personal characteristics of the northern barbarians, and very little in their way of life. He even finds some things objectionable that a lover of liberty in the Tacitean tradition might admire, such as the resolution of the women who slew their children.[1]

So far Strabo might be thought the very model of a cultural nationalist. But he also reveals a very perceptive attitude towards the causes of racial differences. The barbarian is beastly, but only by force of circumstances. He is not beastly in himself. His beastliness is the direct consequence of his economic and physical circumstances. These can change, and as they change the beastliness disappears and the barbarian becomes a civilized man, approved above all if he lives in cities. The recurrent formula is that peace encourages agriculture, and agriculture leads to civic life. In his rather full account of the rashness of Celts in war, Strabo attributes this violence partly to their physical size and partly to their numerous population.[2] These physical advantages encourage what he called their simplicity, which involved them in rash ventures. But given a change of circumstances *politeia*, civic life, emerges, and this leads to *paideia*, civilization.[3] In witness there is not only the famous passage about the role of Massilia in spreading Greek civilization in southern Gaul.[4] In speaking of the violence of the northern

[1] *Ibid.* 3.4.17 (164).
[2] *Ibid.* 4.4.2 (195).
[3] *Ibid.* 4.1.5 (180).
[4] *Ibid.* 4.1.5 (181).

Gauls he concedes that they were capable of listening to rational arguments and to the consideration of advantage to such an extent that they even turn to παιδεία καὶ λόγοι— 'education and arguments'. These terms can only refer to Greek or Roman culture.[1]

So the condition of the barbarian was remediable, and was seen to be continually changing over to what Strabo calls 'our fashion'. This encouraged a liberal attitude of mind towards barbarians, which was not stultified by fear. Strabo was not scared of the barbarians, for the very good reason that they had everywhere been defeated and crushed. He twice remarks significantly upon the inability of the barbarian races to combine against organized armies. Though well aware of the long resistance of the Spanish peoples to Rome, he yet noted the small scale of the operations of the Iberians.[2] They never fitted out a large combination of their powers. If they had been able to unite, Carthage and Rome, he holds, would never have subdued them. Elsewhere, writing of a new and apparently formidable people beyond the Danube, he remarks that barbarian peoples are ineffective against a well trained and well armed phalanx. He instances the utter defeat of some fifty thousand Rhoxolani by a small force of six thousand men, sent against them not by the Romans, but by Mithridates of Pontus.[3]

## Caesar and Ariovistus

A most remarkable example of the deliberate exploitation of national or racial prejudice is provided by Caesar's account of his dealings with Ariovistus, the tribal chief of the Germanic tribe which had established a local empire over

---

[1] *Ibid.* 4.4.2 (195).    [2] *Ibid.* 3.4.5 (158) cf. 4.4.2 (196).
[3] *Ibid.* 7.3.17 (306).

the Sequani and Aedui of northern Gaul. The first book of
Caesar's Gallic wars is one of the most remarkable works of
Latin literature. It has been adversely criticized of recent
years for altogether the wrong reason. Painful and frequently
mistaken efforts have been made to show that it offends
against the goddess of historic truth, as if that were the
primary deity of ancient historical writers. Caesar had other
purposes in this book. In destroying an officially recognized
ally, a *rex socius et amicus populi Romani*, as Ariovistus was,
without formal sanction, Caesar had undoubtedly laid
himself open to a charge of treason. All the art of one of the
most skilful advocates of the day is concentrated on pre-
senting Ariovistus as an impossible person, and in under-
lining Caesar's patience in dealing with a man who was not
prepared to negotiate.

It all begins with a meeting between Caesar and the
Gallic leaders arranged in conditions of great secrecy because
of their fear of Ariovistus. The description of this man is not
given by Caesar himself, but is put in the mouth of the
Gallic noble Diviciacus, who tells how Ariovistus was
oppressing the Sequani and Aedui. A powerful sentence
summarises the aggressive and acquisitive intentions of the
Germans: 'agros et cultum ... Gallorum homines feri ac barbari
adamassent'.[1] To make one barbarian describe another is
doubly effective. Then of Ariovistus himself: ' superbe et
crudeliter imperare, obsides ... poscere ... cruciatus ... edere
si quae res non ad nutum . . . eius facta sit. Hominem
esse barbarum iracundum temerarium'.[2] The basic vices of

[1] Caesar *B.G.* I.31.5. ' The barbarian savages set their hearts on the lands
and products of Gaul.'
[2] *Ibid.* I.31.12–13. ' His orders were arrogant and cruel—a request for
hostages and a threat of torture if things were not done exactly as he bade.
He was a man with a barbarian's hasty passion.'

the barbarian temperament which we have already met in Strabo are given in a few words, the savagery and liability to sudden and unconsidered action. Diviciacus continues: ' We cannot endure his orders any longer . . . but if he learns what we are up to here he will kill all his hostages.' Diviciacus was an Aeduan whose lands were not directly occupied by Ariovistus. The representative of the less fortunate Sequani dared not even open his lips, and sat mute at the conference. Caesar then gives his own reflexions on this state of affairs. He claims to believe that these *homines feri ac barbari* were likely to attack Italy itself, and of Ariovistus in particular he adds: ' tantos sibi spiritus tantam adrogantiam sumpserat ut ferendus non videretur.' [1]

There follows a long account of Caesar's attempted negotiations with Ariovistus, which is meant to illustrate this *adrogantia*. Ariovistus, invited to a colloquy, claimed equality with the Romans. Caesar ought to come to see *him* if he wanted something. Ariovistus could not imagine what Caesar or the Roman people could have to do with *his* Gaul which *he* had conquered.[2] Later Ariovistus, in an exchange of manifestoes, elaborates on the rights of conquest and turns to threats. ' Caesar will learn what is the prowess of the unconquered Germans who in the last fourteen years have not spent a single night under a roof !'[3] Caesar slips in this minor and irrelevant detail in characteristic fashion. The reader is reminded not so much of the toughness as of the savagery of the Germans.

Action follows. Caesar seizes the strong-point of Vesontio and marches into Ariovistus' territory. To underline the

[1] *Ibid.* I.33.5. ' He had assumed such an air of arrogance that he appeared quite intolerable.'

[2] *Ibid.* I.34.2–4.

[3] *Ibid.* I.36.7.

terror inspired by the Germans Caesar inserts the story of the
panic in the Roman camp. Officers and centurions are trying
to secure leave, and the common soldiers are all busy making
their wills.[1] Ariovistus is depicted as coolly treating Caesar's
arrival as a sign that he was accepting Ariovistus's conditions for a colloquy. Caesar takes this without protest. He
comments: 'eum ad sanitatem reverti arbitrabatur ... fore
uti pertinacia desisteret.'[2] These are new terms, not corres-
ponding to anything in Strabo. The Roman objection to the
persistence or obstinacy of their enemy has a considerable
history in other fields.

The colloquy finally takes place, and Ariovistus excels
himself. Caesar ironically remarks: 'Ariovistus ad postulata
Caesaris pauca respondet, de suis virtutibus multa praedi-
cavit.'[3] This brings out the barbarian boastfulness noted by
Strabo. Ariovistus reiterates his rights over *Gallia sua*,
threatens to destroy Caesar to the benefit of his grateful
rivals at Rome, and as a final touch of insolence, advises
Caesar, if he has wars on hand elsewhere, not to trouble
himself, but to leave them all for Ariovistus to manage on his
behalf.[4] The theme is *adrogantia*. Caesar summarizes: 'qua
arrogantia in colloquio Ariovistus usus, omni Gallia Romanis
interdixisset.'[5] He adds a hint of treachery also. He suggests
that Ariovistus meant to trap him by armed force at the
colloquy. Later, when Ariovistus suggests another consul-
tation, Caesar says that he thought it risky to expose any of

[1] *Ibid.* I.39.2–5.
[2] *Ibid.* I.42.2–3. 'He thought Ariovistus was returning to his senses...
and would relax his obstinacy.'
[3] *Ibid.* I.44.1. 'After a short reply to Caesar's demands he made a long
speech about his own abilities.'
[4] *Ibid.* I.44.8–13.
[5] *Ibid* I.46.4. 'At the conference Ariovistus with cool insolence barred
the Romans from the whole of Gaul.'

his officers to the whim of savages, *homines feri*.[1] But he sends two emissaries, the Gaul Procillus and a certain Mettius, a Roman who was a guest friend of Ariovistus. These were both arrested and put in chains by Ariovistus. After the battle, at which Ariovistus was overthrown, Caesar recovered his emissaries. With seeming simplicity he recounts the tale of Procillus, how he had overheard Ariovistus consulting oracles about burning him alive: 'Utrum igni statim necaretur.' Observe the masterly touch of that *statim*. Ariovistus was the sort of man to think nothing of frying an envoy.[2]

The picture is complete—no reader could doubt that Caesar did the right thing when he eliminated Ariovistus. In the narrative the limelight is on Ariovistus himself, while his tribesmen lurk in the background as *homines feri ac barbari*. The terms recur with the regularity of Homeric epithets. In the account of the battles a few barbaric details are thrown in for effect. Superstition forbids the Germans to fight before the new moon, and omens are provided not by respectable magistrates but by the tribal matrons, who attend the battlefield en masse, riding in wagons to urge their menfolk on. The details are selected to shock the Roman mind.[3]

Caesar certainly knew how to exploit prejudice in this field, in the Roman forensic tradition. The effect is comparable to Cicero's attack on the credibility of Gallic witnesses in his defence of the proconsul Fonteius, when he exploits the dark stories about human sacrifice in Gaul to depict the Celts as men utterly lacking in respect for gods or divine sanctions, and hence quite unscrupulous in the observance of

---

[1] *Ibid.* I. 47.3.     [2] *Ibid.* I.53.7.

[3] *Ibid.* I.50.4–5, 51.3.

oaths—throwing in for good measure references to their
outlandish garb, speech and gait.[1] What is remarkable in the
*Bellum Gallicum* is the change of attitude in all the later
books, when Caesar no longer felt the necessity of represent-
ing the enemy in the darkest possible colours. In Book I
Caesar stirred up the most violent prejudice in the forensic
tradition against Ariovistus and his Germans. Summarily, he
said that they were savages characterized by *arrogantia*,
*iracundia*, *temeritas*, *crudelitas* and *perfidia*. But he also
remarks in a much more detached fashion that the Gauls had
been defeated by Ariovistus at the battle of Admagetobriga
because as *homines barbari atque imperiti*, uncivilized peoples
lacking in technique, they could not cope with his superior
strategic cunning.[2] Later Caesar cannot resist attributing to
Ariovistus himself the ironical remark that he was not *tam
barbarum neque tam imperitum rerum*.[3] Caesar gives the show
away. He is thoroughly enjoying himself in this exercise of
misrepresentation, and does not believe a word of it. But for
all that, he knows that there are plenty in his audience who will
believe. So Book I gives a good notion of the contemporary
Roman attitude to the terrible Germans.

## Caesar and the Gauls

In the rest of the *Bellum Gallicum* Caesar no longer had so
strong a motive for misrepresentation. What he says may be
taken to give a more genuine version of Caesar's attitude to
the barbarian world. Where Strabo could not repress a
shudder at the ordinary usages of the barbarians, Caesar is
the cool and detached observer who either in passing com-

---

[1] Cicero, *pro Fonteio* 21–33. Cf. Cicero's treatment of Greeks and Jews,
p. 101.

[2] Caesar *B.G.* I.40.8.

[3] *Ibid.* I. 44.9.

ments or in formal ethnographic descriptions picks out the unusual elements. In Book II, with the conquest of the Belgae, Caesar reckoned he had a good case and did not need to defend his actions. The book is notable for two remarkable tributes to the courage of the enemy, seldom elsewhere the subject of explicit comment. Caesar begins by saying that the Nervii were ' homines feri magnaeque virtutis '.[1] They put up a tremendous fight in difficult terrain, and made a desperate last stand. Caesar is moved to make the warmest comment anywhere in his book, piling on the most unusual superlatives: ' tantae virtutis homines ... transire latissimum flumen, ascendere altissimas ripas, subire iniquissimum locum.' [2] This is followed by a final accolade: ' quae facilia ex difficillimis animi magnitudo redegerat '.[3] It is the only place where Caesar explicitly attributes *animi magnitudo* to his barbarian enemies.

There follows the story of the Atuatuci who, after surrendering on terms, made a treacherous assault upon the Romans. Caesar does not castigate the treachery but notes: ' They fought as brave men must fight in their last chance against an enemy entrenched on higher ground, when their only hope is in their courage.' [4] Nothing derogatory is said about the Nervii or the Atuatuci, but Caesar notes the remarkable impression made by the Roman siege works on a technically backward people. The allies of the Nervii gave in without a fight at the sight of the Roman engines of war: ' Magnitudine

[1] *Ibid.* II.15.5. 'Men savage in their life and of great courage.'

[2] *Ibid.* II.27.5. 'They were indeed men of courage to cross a river of great breadth, assail banks of great steepness, and assault a most unfavourable position.'

[3] *Ibid.* II.27.5. Cf. VII.52.4 for *animi magnitudo* as the virtue of the Roman soldier. 'Their greatness of heart made hard things easy for them.'

[4] *Ibid.* II.33.4.

operum quae neque viderant ante Galli neque audierant.' [1]
So too the Atuatuci. First they jeered at the siege tower
which was being built out of range of their walls. But when
it began to move forward they were panic-stricken, and
reckoned that the gods must be helping the Romans to move
such enormous things so fast.[2] These incidents were not lost
on Caesar. In Britain he deliberately used his long ships as a
terror weapon: ' species barbaris inusitatior '.[3] Hence too
came the notion of bridging the Rhine to impress the
Germanic tribes.[4] Such seems to be the meaning of the
strange remark in Book IV that a crossing by boats would be
contrary to the *dignitas* of himself and the Roman people, and
that he would cross by a bridge or not at all, despite the
difficulty of the operation. It becomes part of Caesar's state-
craft to overawe the barbarians by demonstrations of superior
technique. This is the correlate of Caesar's continual assump-
tion that the barbarians are *imperiti*. Because of this sense of
superiority the question of racial feeling inspired by fear
simply did not arise.

Caesar also admired the barbarian toughness and endurance
of harsh conditions of life. He notes the extreme tolerance of
cold by the Suebi and makes an unusual observation about
their huge physique. This he attributes partly to their diet of
meat and milk and to their continual exercise, but partly also
to their freedom of life, in that from boyhood their actions
were not determined by *officium* and *disciplina*, civil obliga-
tions and rules of society. Instead, ' nihil omnino contra

[1] *Ibid.* II.12.5. 'At the vastness of the machines which Gauls had never
seen or heard of before.'

[2] *Ibid.* II.30.3–4, 31.1–2.

[3] *Ibid.* IV.25.1. Cf. IV.25.2. 'Inusitato genere tormentorum permoti
barbari.' 'A sight outside the experience of barbarians.'

[4] *Ibid.* IV.17.1.

voluntatem faciant '.[1] The difference between Caesar and the pupil of Posidonius is remarkable. Strabo's ultimate criterion was τὸ πολιτικόν, the machinery of civic life. But *officium* and *disciplina* have no necessary connection with cities.

Caesar has other things to say that are more in line with Strabo. He too notes the *temeritas* of the Gauls, their sudden decisions for action, and their sudden changes of purpose. This he explains as largely conditioned by the inadequacy of their intelligence services. He remarks rather scornfully: 'Incertis rumoribus serviant.'[2] His strongest statement concerns the Aedui, whose late and nearly fatal desertion of his side was largely induced by false information. They were motivated by 'avaritia . . . iracundia et temeritas quae maxime illi hominum generi est innata '. This *temeritas* consisted in a readiness to treat street corner gossip—*levis auditio*—as a *res comperta*.[3] This is the most biting criticism that Caesar makes of any Gauls—*illud hominum genus*. But too much should not be read into it. It turns up in milder terms in his account of the deception of the Venelli by his legate Titurius, who infiltrated false information among them that he was about to abandon his camp. This induced them to stage an assault. Caesar laconically comments: 'Fere libenter homines id quod volunt credunt.'[4] That is a remark about human nature in general. But when the attack of the Venelli failed they lost heart and came to terms. Caesar comments again, in the strain of Strabo: 'The Gallic mentality was ready and eager to rush into wars, but very bad at enduring defeats.'[5]

[1] *Ibid.* IV.1.8–9. 'They do nothing at all against their inclination.'
[2] *Ibid.* IV.5.3. 'They are the slaves of baseless rumours.' Cf. VI.20.1–2.
[3] *Ibid.* VII.42.2. 'Greed, passionate anger and the rashness that is inborn in that sort of men.'
[4] *Ibid.* III.18.6. 'Men generally believe readily what they want to believe.'
[5] *Ibid.* III.19.6.

These are the only passages where Caesar speaks with deliberate contempt of the Gauls. He pays them one notable compliment when describing the defence of Avaricum against the Roman engineers. ' Est summae genus sollertiae atque ad omnia imitanda et efficienda quae a quoque traduntur aptissimum '[1]—' They are a folk extremely skilful at adapting other people's inventions.' Though Caesar has occasion to mention certain Gallic tricks that could have been dressed up as perfidy he seldom bothers to do so. It is his soldiers who label the massacre of Romans at Cenabum as treachery.[2] He records two similar massacres that took place after safe conduct had been given with no stronger condemnation than the adverb *crudeliter*.[3] He notes in some detail the severity of the discipline of Vercingetorix—cutting off of ears, gouging out of eyes, executions by fire. Caesar comments with a touch of irony ' his suppliciis celeriter coacto exercitu '— ' By mass tortures he quickly raised an army.'[4] In the account of the rising of Vercingetorix Caesar seems to avoid the elaboration of prejudice as positively as he exploited it in the first book. There is an element of conscious superiority in Caesar's mind, but he deliberately suppresses it. His cool attitude is shown by an incident when the Aedui, still faithful to Caesar, send aid to the Bituriges against Vercingetorix. The force returns without making contact, alleging fear of an ambush. Caesar remarks: ' Whether this was for the reason which they reported or out of treachery I could not discover and therefore will assert nothing definite.'[5] After Book I it is generally Caesar's way to let the facts speak for themselves.

[1] *Ibid.* VII.22.1.
[2] *Ibid.* VII.17.7. Contrast VII.3.1, where there is no comment.
[3] *Ibid.* VII.38.9. Cf. V.34–37.
[4] *Ibid.* VII.4.10, 5.1.
[5] *Ibid.* VII.5.6.

Hence his impersonal account of Vercingetorix, saying nothing overt by way of praise or blame, which has so offended Celtic nationalists in modern times. They are quite mistaken. Set against Caesar's account of Ariovistus in Book I his version of the last words of Vercingetorix: ' Id bellum se suscepisse non suarum necessitatum sed communis libertatis causa ... et quoniam sit fortunae cedendum, ad utramque rem se illis offerre seu morte sua Romanis satisfacere seu vivum tradere velint.' [1] That is a great tribute to greatness. There is no touch of either condescension or contempt as between Roman and barbarian.

The epitaph places in the centre the theme of *libertas*. Caesar, unlike Tacitus in his account of the Britains, does not make a great splash about *libertas*. But he fairly puts it in evidence at the beginnings of Books II and III that the Gauls were fighting for their freedom, and that subjection to Rome meant *servitus*. The cause of the Venetic revolt is ' Ut in ea libertate quam a maioribus acceperint permanere ... mallent '.[2] Though Caesar also alleged the *mobilitas* and *levitas* of the Gauls, these ethnic considerations are secondary, and he generalizes the theme in terms of human nature again: ' Omnes ... homines natura libertati studere et condicionem servitutis odisse.' [3] So too with the great revolts of Books V and VII the recovery of the ancestral freedom is put clearly as the motive, though the causes are much mixed up, in their earlier stages, with the ambitions and disap-

[1] *Ibid*. VII.89.1–2. 'He had undertaken the war not for his own needs but for the freedom of all. As he must now yield to fortune he offers himself to them to use as they like, either to appease the Romans by his death or to hand him over alive.'

[2] *Ibid*. III.8.4. ' They preferred to remain in the condition of freedom which they had inherited from their ancestors.'

[3] *Ibid*. III.10.3. ' It is the nature of all men to aim at freedom and hate the status of slavery.'

pointments of certain Gallic notables. Very characteristically, in discussing the secession of the Senones, Caesar begins by saying: ' It sufficed with a barbarian folk that a few leaders of revolt should come forward.' But he goes on to add: ' Yet the general rebellion was not surprising considering that the folk who used to be reckoned the most warlike in the world were aggrieved by the thought that they had lost their reputation, and were subservient to the orders of Rome.' [1]

Caesar reserved the development of this theme for the very end of Book VII, where he gives it a remarkable exposition in the speech of Critognatus at Alesia. Critognatus contrasts Roman imperialism, as revealed by the permanent exploitation and provincialization of southern Gaul (Gallia Narbonensis) unfavourably with the former temporary devastation of the country by the Cimbri.[2] These left the Gauls in the free possession of their land and customs, but the Romans wanted everything. This is a remarkable piece of self-criticism from a Roman pen. It is, after all, Caesar who chooses to write thus.

The *libertas* theme keeps very odd company in the speech of Critognatus. Caesar introduces the speech with a remark-ably hostile criticism: ' I must not omit the speech of Crito-gnatus', he writes, 'on account of its *singularis et nefaria crude-litas*'—its unimaginable atrocity. A very rhetorical passage on the necessity of endurance in the cause of freedom leads up to the suggestion that the besieged should maintain life by practising selective cannibalism until the relief force arrived.[3] This is the one place in the *Bellum Gallicum* where Caesar seems positively to be shocked out of his normally tolerant and open-minded attitude towards the barbarians. Yet the

---

[1] *Ibid.* V.54.4–5.      [2] *Ibid.* VII.77.14–15.
[3] *Ibid.* VII.77.2, 12.

condemnation is only of Critognatus, not of the Gauls as such. Caesar notes that the Gauls too were shocked, and adopted the advice only as a last resort. Caesar's intention in giving the Critognatus speech is enigmatic. It is the only set speech in *oratio recta* in Books II to VII, and it is set with great effect at the moment of supreme crisis. The speech reminds us of all that was at stake at Alesia in terms that leave crystal clear the nature of Roman imperialism. We are bidden admire Gauls for their resolution, and at the same time we are meant to shudder at the darker side of barbarism.

## Caesar's formal ethnologia

I have deliberately left out of account so far Caesar's formal description of the Gauls and Germans in Book VI. This is not because I think that Caesar did not write most of them, or that he did not describe his own observations, but because his incidental comments in the main narrative are much more informative about his own judgment.[1] Even by the standard of the *Bellum Gallicum*, the presentation of the facts in this part of VI is remarkably cool and detached. Caesar gives it as his intention ' to discuss the customs of Gallia and Germania and how these tribes differ from one another '.[2] He writes much more fully about the Gauls, but limits himself to three aspects, internal politics, religious usage, and family life. The information is very unevenly distributed. Under the first head he comments in some detail on the internal factions that divide Gaul as a whole and each separate tribe,[3] and the system of *clientela* which was

---

[1] This is not the place for a discussion on possible interpolations in Book VI. Probably only the sections on animals and the Hercynian forest (VI.25–28) are such.

[2] *Ibid.* VI.11.1.

[3] *Ibid.* 11–12.

the basis of the power of individuals.[1] He says nothing about economic life, and nothing about political institutions except for the Druids.[2] He treats them at great length, but is primarily concerned with their political power and institutions. He is brief over their religious functions, though aware that their power depended on religious sanctions. His summary of their beliefs is in terms of philosophical rather than of religious ideas. Caesar in fact separates the section on the Druids from his account of Gallic religion by a chapter about the political role of the Gallic nobility.[3] In the discussion of religion his attention is concentrated on the place of human sacrifice both in public and private life, and on the strong taboos that protected the great treasures stored in the shrines of the gods.

In his account of family life he picks out peculiarities in the system of doweries and in the subjection of the wife to the kinsmen of the husband.[4] He notes the peculiar custom that fathers did not admit their immature children to their presence in public.[5] He notes also the ostentation of Celtic funerals, and describes at length the obsolescent custom of immolating favourite servants on the pyre.[6]

Caesar is picking out the ways in which the Gauls differ, not from the Germans as he proposed, but from what he calls ' other peoples ', evidently the Romans and Greeks.[7] It is difficult to detect what Caesar thought of the customs that he describes. There is a notable absence of comment, but the selection of material may indicate Caesar's interest if not his

---

[1] *Ibid.* 13.1–2, 15.1–2.      [2] *Ibid.* 13.4–14, if 14 is Caesarian.
[3] *Ibid.* 15, ' equites ', preceding religion in 16–17.
[4] *Ibid.* 19.1–3.       [5] *Ibid.* 18.3.
[6] *Ibid.* 19.4–5.
[7] *Ibid.* 17.2, and 18.3, in connexion with treatment of children and opinions about the gods.

valuation. This must be true at least of his stress on the realities rather than the formalities of political power, and perhaps of the choice of minor details, such as the rather long description of the method of reckoning time.[1] The inclusion of a summary of Druidic theory, as Caesar understood it, may be significant.[2] Strabo touched on this in general terms, but Caesar particularizes. The concentration on the horrific element in religious usages and funeral customs may suggest, with the parallel of the Critognatus speech, that Caesar was appalled by these things, and especially by the cremation of the living.[3] He underlines the point that though detected criminals were preferred for these purposes, if they were not available the Druids resort (*descendunt*) to the execution of the innocent.[4] This seems to be a value judgment. Elsewhere the only personal comment is not an evaluation, when Caesar attributes the refusal of the Druids to record their teaching in writing partly to secrecy and partly to the fear of weakening the faculty of memory.[5]

In a final footnote Caesar describes the method taken in certain tribal states to protect decisions on public policy from the influence of idle rumour—that Gallic weakness noted elsewhere as disastrous. Such states, he says, were thought to manage their affairs well, while those who were moved by rumours were *homines temerarii atque imperiti*, disapproving terms used elsewhere.[6] But this passage is as enigmatic as the rest. Caesar may be giving his own approval, but the terms are attributed to his informant: ' existimantur '

---

[1] *Ibid.* 18.2. 'They reckon time by the number not of days but of nights.' Caesar's interest in time reckoning is shown by his reform of the calendar.

[2] *Ibid.* 14.5–6.                    [3] *Ibid.* 16.3–5.

[4] *Ibid.* 16.5.                       [5] *Ibid.* 14.4.

[6] *Ibid.* VI 20.1–3. 'Men of sudden action through inexperience.'

and ' cognitum est '—' my information is to this effect '.

Something of special interest emerges from this section. The Gauls are described in terms of Roman usage, not just linguistically because Caesar is writing in Latin, but organically. They are viewed as a people whose civilization, though different in many customs, and barbaric in some, was yet of the same general pattern as Caesar's own. The Celts may be a *natio admodum dedita religionibus*,[1] but their gods were like the Roman gods. ' De his eandem fere quam reliquae gentes habent opinionem.'[2] The differences in usages of ordinary life which Caesar notes concern matters of dowries, *patria potestas* and funerals.[3] The details or the species differ, but the pattern is the same. Caesar, like Strabo, sees no absolute gulf between Roman and Gaul, though he sees enough to mark the Gauls off as a separate species within the genus. The Druids stand out as the most distinctive phenomenon, and it is noteworthy that though Caesar uses many technical terms of Roman judicial life in describing the political activity of the Druids,[4] yet in explaining their religious functions he uses no Latin word that would equate them with the Roman priestly colleges of which he was the supreme head as *pontifex maximus*. Such terms might well have been handy in explaining, for example, the role of the supreme Druid.[5] But the Druids as priests were not ' like us ', and Caesar was certainly not going to equate their chief witch-doctor with his own august office.

---

[1] *Ibid*. 16.1. ' A people greatly given to superstition.'

[2] *Ibid*. 17.2. ' They have much the same opinion about them as other folk do.'

[3] *Ibid*. 19.1–5.

[4] *Ibid*. 13.5: 'de omnibus controversiis ... constituunt ... decernunt'. *Ibid*. 13.10: ' decretis iudiciisque parent '.

[5] *Ibid*. 13.8–9.

Caesar then sees the Gauls as a barbarian people with some unpleasant and several extraordinary customs, but also as one whose ways were not of a totally different order from that of the Graeco-Roman world: *homines imperiti* and *barbari*, but not *feri*. That epithet is reserved for the Germans, and applied by Caesar only to the Belgic Nervii, whom he reckoned most akin of all the Gauls to the Germanic folk.[1]

## Caesar and the Germans

It is far otherwise with Caesar's account of the Germans in Book VI. This is only three chapters long, compared with ten devoted to the Gauls.[2] He soon disposes of the difference between Gauls and Germans. ' They have no Druids and no sacrifices and no gods like the Celtic gods.'[3] That is all. The rest of the account bears no relation to the description of Gallic culture. The topics selected are quite different. Most space is given to the economic and agrarian system, to tribal leadership in war, and to the method of tribal raids, interspersed with sociological observations about sex, customs and guest-friends. The total effect is of a people who are different in all their usages and organization, or lack of it, from the pattern of the Celtic and the Graeco-Roman world alike. There are no similarities and no points of contact. Caesar as usual makes no positive comments, but stylistically the sense of alienation comes out very strongly in a series of negative sentences:[4] ' deorum ... reliquos ne fama quidem acceperunt ... agriculturae non student ... neque quisquam

[1] Above p. 19, and *B.G.* II.4.1, 8.

[2] *Ibid.* 21–23.

[3] *Ibid.* 21.1–2, summarized.

[4] *Ibid.* 21.2, 22.1–2, 23.5–6. ' They know nothing of the other gods ... have no serious agriculture ... no separate ownership of land ... no common government ... brigandage is no crime,' etc.

agri modum certum ... habet ... in pace nullus est communis magistratus ... latrocinia nullam habent infamiam.'

Caesar was particularly surprised at the communal system of land tenure.[1] He shows this by offering a series of explanations, five in number. These are all variants on two themes. The first is that permanent ownership would lead to the accumulation of wealth and destroy the social and political unity of the tribe by introducing faction. The second is that permanent ownership would diminish physical hardihood and zest for war. Caesar puts these explanations forward as the Germans' own. But he regards them as valid, and they give a definition of German tribal life as something *sui generis*, based on economic independence at subsistence level, social equality, and patriarchal leadership, a system geared to continual warfare in the effort to keep their lands. That is in complete contrast to Caesar's picture of Gallic society, in which wealthy feudal lords, controlling private armies of serfs, in a state of economic dependence, struggle for political supremacy within their tribal regions.

The contrast is there, but Caesar does not underline it. He ends his survey by drawing attention to the condition of the Volcae Tectosages, a Gallic people who had established themselves in the heart of the southern Germanic area. He remarks that because the Volcae live in the same economic conditions as the Germanic tribes, their pattern of life and personal physique and condition is the same as that of the Germans.[2] He contrasts them with the Celts of Gallia, who had developed their economic life through the propinquity of the Roman province and its supplies of consumer goods, and who gradually lost their supremacy in the skills of war.[3] So he

[1] *Ibid.* 22.3–4.      [2] *Ibid.* 24.2–5.
[3] *Ibid.* 24.5–6.

ends by saying, like Strabo, that the Gauls had once been like what the Germans still were, and attributes the difference to an economic, not a racial, cause.

There is an earlier and briefer account of Germanic customs in the description of the Suebi in Book IV. Caesar there omits the topics of religion, leadership and marriage customs, and concentrates on the economic pattern and its consequences.[1] The general lines, and some details are the same as in Book VI: the community of land, the predominance of stock-keeping, the annual war raids, the isolation of tribal territories, and the physical toughness, illustrated by some details not repeated in VI, the bareback riding, the inadequate clothing. Caesar develops a theme that only appears by implication in VI, the virtual absence of *mercatores*, itinerant traders from the Mediterranean world. The Germans desire no imports, and have no interest even in draught animals of quality.[2] He contrasts this with the passion of the Gallic nobles for bloodstock. Equally the Germans will not import wine, and Caesar gives a reason that recurs in another context of communal ownership. They reckoned that wine made men soft and effeminate.[3] Caesar finishes the account of the Suebi with an example analogous to the role of the Volcae Tectosages in VI. He describes the condition of the Ubii, whose territory lay between the Suebi and Gaul. They were, he says, a Suebic people, with a difference: ' eiusdem generis sed ceteris humaniores ', i.e. more like civilized men.[4] The reason was that their territory

[1] *Ibid.* IV.1–3.
[2] *Ibid.* IV.2.1–2.
[3] *Ibid.* IV.2.6. The Belgic Nervii likewise refuse wine as effeminate, II.15.4.
[4] *Ibid.* IV.3.3–4.

lay open to traders from south of the Rhine and to Celtic influence. But the consequence was that they were reduced to the condition of tributary subjects by the other Suebic folk.

As with the general narrative of Books II–VI, so too in the formal ethnography of IV and VI, Caesar gives a remarkably unprejudiced account of both cultures with even less indication of approval or disapproval. But one can discern that he realized the extreme otherness of the Germanic way of life, and the close affinity of Gallic usage to Graeco-Roman practices, even if he occasionally concedes a shudder or a condescending smile at some Celtic puerility or barbarism.

# 2

# TACITUS AND THE BARBARIANS

In my last lecture I discussed the attitude of Caesar and Strabo to the northern barbarians. Briefly, it seemed that Strabo had a general dislike of barbarian culture, and a horror of savages, but regarded the barbarian condition as capable of assimilation to the Graeco-Roman model in favourable circumstances. He approved of assimilated barbarians, though as a good Hellenistic man he thought this possible only in a city environment. Caesar had a broader outlook, was much less disapproving of a culture merely because it was different, and could admire barbarians for heroic virtues. But he had an equally strong objection to manifestations of savagery. He drew a clear distinction between barbarians whose culture or organization was not widely different from the Roman pattern, and *feri*, wild men or savages. Another novelty found in Caesar was the clear but occasional emergence of the idea that the Gauls were fighting against the Romans for freedom.

These two pointers lead through from Caesar to the third great witness, Tacitus. But before I turn to him I would draw attention to the opinion of a plain and direct man, Velleius Paterculus, the amateur historian. Velleius had practical experience of the Germanic tribes at the height of their conflict with Rome, as an officer of the relief force that came to the Rhine after the great disaster of Varus in A.D. 9. He has no good word to say for the Germans in his short account of these events. To him they are absolute savages, *feri*, who had nothing human about them except their physical form and the faculty of speech. He uses *feritas*

33

*Germana* as a proverbial term,[1] and ridicules Varus for imagining that such men could be governed by the usages of law.[2] This is all the more interesting because he writes rather differently about the Pannonians, admitting their possibilities for civilization, and commenting on the spread of Latin among them.[3] Yet the great Pannonian revolt which he describes was no less dangerous for Rome than that of Arminius and the Germans. The difference is that Velleius has been present in Germany, and in his shrill tone of abuse one may detect the authentic hysteria of personal fear, even if recollected in tranquillity.

After Velleius and Strabo the next witness is Cornelius Tacitus a century later, since the elder Pliny is surprisingly silent on the topic of this enquiry. In Tacitus' historical books, and in the *Germania*, if its author is in truth Tacitus, there is a change of attitude due to the passage of time. The barbarian Germans and Britons are no longer new and strange. The threat that they posed to Rome has been overcome or more accurately assessed, and the writers can take them for granted in a way that Strabo and Caesar could not. The element of horror and fear that they inspire has diminished and become conventional. Instead, they tend to be represented in a somewhat false light as the representatives of virtues that the writers admired or sought in vain in their own society. This tendency is very much stronger because, unless I am much mistaken, the writers are working at second hand. It is difficult to believe that Tacitus and the author of the *Germania* have seen the barbarians with their own eyes, like Caesar and Velleius. Hence a glow of literary and political prejudice colours the picture.

---

[1] Velleius 2.106.2, 119.5.  [2] *Ibid.* 2.117.3–4.
[3] *Ibid.* 2.110.5.

In the *Germania* this tendency is only partial. The attitude of the author is much more complex than is often realized. It is a commonplace to speak of the author idealizing the German tribes. But this is true only of certain aspects of barbarian life. In the first part of the *Germania* the author gives a remarkably detailed account of the social and political life of the Germans as a whole, treating religion, in Roman fashion, as a part of politics.[1] The author's praises are concentrated on matrimonial and sexual customs.[2] He also approves the absence of luxury in specific things, notably food, funerals and the acquisition of consumer goods, and the absence of usury.[3] He seems also to approve the management of feuds and guest-friendships, and the repression of freedmen.[4] But a great deal is given without positive comment, and there is much that the author disapproves, such as the lack of energy and purpose in times of peace: ' ipsi hebent . . . ament inertiam et oderint quietem '.[5] Hence he thinks little of the backward state of agriculture and the inadequacy of housing, due to *inscitia aedificandi*.[6] He criticizes severely the tendency to drunkenness, and the reckless gambling: ' ea est in re prava pervicacia '.[7]

But one must not take the appearance of praise and blame too literally. The author will sacrifice a good deal for the

[1] *Germ.* 7.2–3, 10, 11.4. The accuracy of Tacitus' observations is the theme of modern commentaries, such as J. G. Anderson, *Corneli Taciti De origine et situ Germanorum* (Oxford, 1938), and of studies like that of E. A. Thompson (cited p. 1 n. 1), while the attitude of Tacitus, apart from his supposed idealization of the Germans, eludes detailed comment, e.g. in R. Syme, *Tacitus* (Oxford, 1962), and G. Walser, *Rom, das Reich, und die fremden Völker . . . der frühen Kaiserzeit* (Berlin, 1951). But E. Paratore, *Tacito*[2] (Roma, 1962), 228 ff., discusses the Tacitean portrait critically and at length, though inclining to the idealistic interpretation.

[2] *Germ.* 17.4, 19.3–4, 20.3.  
[3] *Ibid.* 5.4–5, 26.1, 27.  
[4] *Ibid.* 21.1–3, 25.3.  
[5] *Ibid.* 15.1.  
[6] *Ibid.* 14.5, 26.2.  
[7] *Ibid.* 22.2., 23.2, 24.3–4.

sake of a clever *sententia* or witticism in the style fashionable in contemporary oratory—as in the famous description of the Germanic method of taking counsel: ' deliberant dum fingere nesciunt, constituunt dum errare non possunt '.[1] So too about funeral mourning: ' feminis lugere honestum est, viris meminisse '.[2] Allowing for the love of a good *sententia*, and the lengthy list of things disapproved, the author's attitude is much more ambivalent than is commonly supposed. The same duality of judgment is apparent in the second part of the book, which describes the separate tribes.

The Semnones are picked upon for their addiction to human sacrifice and other superstitious practices,[3] a theme very lightly touched in the first part, while the Chauci are given credit at some length for what the author calls their *iustitia*.[4] This means their unaggressive attitude to their neighbours: they are *sine cupiditate sine impotentia*, strong terms. The Cherusci, with similar characteristics, provide material for an extended *sententia* at their expense, to the effect that *modestia* and *probitas* are merely *nomina superioris*.[5] The greatest commendation is reserved for the Chatti—one of Rome's most dangerous contemporary enemies. They are commended not for barbarian virtues, but for qualities of rationality and organization that are essentially Roman: ' Multum ut inter Germanos rationis ac sollertiae ... quodque rarissimum nec nisi Romanae disciplinae concessum plus

---

[1] *Ibid.* 22.4. ' They take counsel when in no condition to feign their thoughts, and made their decisions when free from the possibility of error.'

[2] *Ibid.* 27.2. ' They think it honourable for women to mourn the dead, and for men to remember them.'

[3] *Ibid.* 39.2.

[4] *Ibid.* 35.2–3.

[5] *Ibid.* 36.1. ' Honesty and moderation are titles claimed by superior force.'

reponere in duce quam in exercitu.' [1] This tribute is far from
idealization. It does not prevent the author from explaining
in terms of revulsion the strange usages of the Chattan
champion fighters, who did not cut off their hair or put off
their iron bracelets until they had killed their first man, and
who spent their lives in savage idleness at the expense of
others: ' prodigi alieni contemptores sui ', another *sententia*
and an unfriendly one.[2]

These were the Germans best known to the Romans
through warfare. Worse follows as the author turns to
remoter peoples. In eastern Suebia lie the Harii, who stain
themselves black and fight by night. They are described in
the language of horror.[3] Beyond are the Sitones, who incur
a hostile *sententia* for being ruled by a woman: ' etiam a
servitute degenerant '.[4] The Langobardi across the Elbe have
a splendid festival of Nerthus, marred by the custom of
slaying the attendants of the goddess.[5] The Aestii of the
Baltic zone are commended for agricultural industry and for
picking amber,[6] but criticized for not investigating its
origins: ' nec quae . . . ratio gignat ut barbaris quaesitum '—
the phrase reveals the usual scoff of the superior man.[7]
Finally come the peoples beyond Suebia, of whom the author
can say little good, Peucini, Venedi and Fenni. ' Sordes
omnium ac torpor.'[8] The Fenni are the strangest.[9] They
still lived in the Stone Age, it seems, and used bone instead of
iron for cutting edges. ' Mira feritas, foeda paupertas.'

---

[1] *Ibid.* 30.2. ' For a Germanic people they are much given to orderly
thought and technique. They have more confidence in their military leaders
than in the armed mass, a quality characteristic of Roman organization.'

[2] *Ibid.* 31.1–2, 5.          [3] *Ibid.* 43.6.(5)

[4] *Ibid.* 45.9.               [5] *Ibid.* 40.5.

[6] *Ibid.* 45.4.               [7] *Ibid.* 45.5.

[8] *Ibid.* 46.1. ' All live in filth and sloth.'    [9] *Ibid.* 46.3–5.

Absolute beasts, they eat grass or hunt animals for subsistence, and live in wattle huts or nests. The author ends
on a strange note, with a touch of ethical philosophy. ' Sed
beatius arbitrantur quam ingemere agris, inlaborare domibus.'[1]
They have secured the ideal existence, and have no need of
prayers, ' securi adversus homines, securi adversus deos '.
But the comment is ironical, not idealizing. The author does
not care for them at all.

The Germans come decidedly less well out of the second
part of the *Germania* than out of the first. The nearest and
best known receive most commendation. The remoter
peoples are full of horrors, including what the author calls
*superstitio*, a bad word in Flavian writers, and new in the
context of barbarian ideology. It is applied to the Semnones
and their sacred grove—' eo . . . omnis superstitio respicit '
—to the Baltic Aestii who wore strange amulets, *insigne
superstitionis*, and to the brother-gods of the Nahanarvoli.[2]
The author is again less kind in this detailed survey than in
the first part, where the Germans received credit for not
having images or houses for their gods.[3]

The partial and limited approval of the barbarians in the
*Germania* may be compared to the rather curious account
that the elder Pliny gives of the people of Taprobene, the
ancient Ceylon. It is odd that the factual Pliny, who had
served for long periods on the Rhine and in Spain as an
officer and procurator, is never moved to any comment on
the European barbarians of whom he gives such long and
accurate lists in his geography, yet bursts out when he has

---

[1] 'They reckon this a happier existence than groaning over lands and
sweating over houses.'

[2] *Ibid.* 39.4, 45.3, 43.5. For Flavian usage cf. Pliny, *Epp.* 6.2.2, 10.96.8;
Tac. *Agric.* 11.4, *Hist.* 4.61.2, cited p. 48 n. 3.

[3] *Ibid.* 9.3.

passed far beyond the limits of the Roman world to tell strange stories about Hyperboreans and Indians. Here at last in his account of Taprobene we have the myth of the innocent barbarian.[1] Pliny contrasts these people with the Romans in terms of wealth and justice.[2] They dwell in exile beyond the civilized world, *extra orbem relegata*, and hence are mainly free from Roman vices.[3] They have gold and precious stones but do not use them to excess. They have no slaves, and they do not waste working hours by sleeping during daylight. The cost of living is stable ('annonam non augeri'), they have no civil law suits, and though it seems that crimes are not unknown they have a splendid system of criminal jurisdiction. Their lands are well cultivated, they hunt tigers, and live for a hundred years. This is a very curious mixture of ideas, blending philosophical speculations about Eutopias, like that of Euhemerus, with travellers' information about the far east, spiced with Pliny's known prejudices about certain Roman failings.[4] The characteristic thing is that this paradise is situated far beyond the peoples with whom the Romans were in familiar contact—a single Roman freedman is known to have visited Ceylon in very unusual circumstances.[5] The people of Taprobene belong to a race that had had no possible affiliation with the barbarians of north Europe. Pliny would agree with the author of the *Germania* in not locating paradise in north Germany,

---

[1] Pliny, *Nat. Hist.* 6.89–90.

[2] *Ibid.* 89.

[3] Pliny characteristically says that they were not free from such vices, and then illustrates the opposite.

[4] For the elder Pliny's use of time see Pliny, *Epp.* 3.5.8, 10, 13; for his disapproval of gold, *N.H.* 33.4–8, 42, 48.

[5] For the voyage of the freedman of Plocamus to Ceylon see *Nat. Hist.* 6.84–5.

but disagrees in finding virtue only in the most remote barbarians.

The *Germania* as a whole has no consistent theoretical attitude towards the barbarians. The idealization of the virtuous barbarian is limited to aspects of Germanic life that provided a legitimate contrast with the contemporary vices of Roman society, including even that hardy perpetual of the satirists, legacy hunting, or *captatio*.[1] The author otherwise remains a true ethnologist, noting the facts as he proceeds. In several places he makes it clear that he had in his mind a definition of barbarian culture much like that of Strabo. The various barbarians are to be distinguished either *sermone cultu sede* or *sermone institutis moribus*.[2] The Fenni have houses, use shields and move on foot.[3] Therefore (he thinks) they cannot be Sarmatians, who live in wagons and ride horses. The Osi cannot be Germanic because they speak Pannonian and pay tribute, a non-Germanic thing.[4] The narrative proceeds strictly within the prescribed terms.

While the author certainly admires the barbarians for the virtues which he thinks they possess, these were not barbarian virtues of courage and toughness, as in Caesar, but those ancient civilized virtues of which Roman writers had long been deploring their own loss. Purely barbarian usage and organization receive no commendation—the *comitatus*,[5] the champion fighters,[6] the system of punishment,[7] the taking of omens,[8] housing and clothing,[9] are all described at length in neutral terms. The one German people to be commended

---

[1] *Germ.* 20.5.
[2] *Ibid.* 28.3, 46.1. Cf. the passage of the elder Pliny cited p. 57 n. 2.
[3] *Ibid.* 46.1.  [4] *Ibid.* 43.1.
[5] *Ibid.* 13.3–14.4.  [6] *Ibid.* 31.1–4.
[7] *Ibid.* 12.  [8] *Ibid.* 10.
[9] *Ibid.* 16, 17.1–3.

for its public life was the tribe whose usages dimly resembled the Roman discipline.[1]

A theme that plays a very minor part in the *Germania* is the topic of *libertas*. Political liberty is barely mentioned thrice, and in the shortest and least significant contexts.[2] Each time it occurs in a *sententia* commenting upon an institution, such as the role of freedmen: ' apud ceteros impares libertini libertatis argumentum sunt '.[3] The Germans are not feted as the living embodiment of *libertas*, nor as its champions in their wars against Rome. It is in this that the *Germania* differs so widely from the treatment that Tacitus gives to the Germans, Gauls and Britons in his *Agricola, Histories* and *Annals*. Where the Germanic wars of Rome are mentioned in the *Germania*, it is not the success of the Germans in defending their freedom but the threat to Roman security that is underlined.[4] The well-known phrases ' tam diu Germania vincitur ' and ' triumphati magis quam victi ' give the theme. The author is indifferent to the achievements of the Cherusci under Arminius.[5] They appear oddly in the role of virtuous barbarians, *olim boni aequique Cherusci*, while the long elaboration of the Germanic peril in ch. 37 is developed from a reference to the Cimbri, and the war of 105–1 B.C. This is a far remove from Tacitus' great tribute in the *Annals* to Arminius as the true liberator of Germany from Rome at the height of her power.[6]

This indifference of the *Germania* to the freedom theme calls in question the Tacitean authorship, because this theme

[1] Above p. 36–7.
[2] *Germ.* 21.1, 25.3, 45.9.
[3] ' The unequal status of freedmen is elsewhere a demonstration of liberty.'
[4] *Ibid.* 33.2, 37.2, 37.6.
[5] *Ibid.* 36.2.
[6] Tac. *Ann.* 2.88.

is not only the *leitmotiv* of all Tacitus' other writings but looms particularly large in his treatment of barbarians. This trait appears straightway and most forcibly in the *Agricola*, apparently written and certainly completed in the same year as the *Germania*.[1] The dominant pattern in Tacitus is the treatment of the barbarian *dux belli* as a *vindex libertatis*. The representation is formalized by the provision of set speeches which enlarge on the theme of subservience and liberation. In the *Agricola* no less than four out of forty-six chapters are devoted to this theme: one in indirect speech gives the thoughts of Boudicca, and three are allocated to the direct eloquence of Calgacus.[2] This is the extreme instance in Tacitus. In the *Histories* he alters his technique. *Libertas* is the theme of the large part of Book IV allocated to the revolt of Civilis and Classicus. But Tacitus is much briefer in the presentation of the theme of freedom here than in the *Agricola*. He opens the story with a twelve-line summary of a speech of Civilis about liberty akin to the material in the *Agricola*.[3] This is followed up in ch. 32 by a similar exhortation of the same length in direct speech, and later by a summary of a deliberation on the same topics between the leaders.[4] More space is given to a novel version of the old theme, when the free German Tencteri appeal to the half-Romanized and subject Ubii to throw off their shackles.[5] But when the council of the Gauls meets to consider the situation there is not even a summary of the *meditata oratio* which Tacitus says was given by the rebel leaders.[6] He merely remarks that it

---

[1] *Germ.* 37.2, *Agric.* 3.1. Cf. Syme, *Tacitus* i.19, 46. If the authorship of the *Germania* is not to be doubted, the difference of emphasis is all the more remarkable.

[2] *Agric.* 15, 30–32.   [3] *Hist.* 4.14, 2–4.

[4] *Ibid.* 4.55.4.   [5] *Ibid.* 64.

[6] *Ibid.* 68.4.

consisted of ' all the complaints commonly brought against great empires ', and concentrates instead on the arguments of the pro-Roman opposition.[1] In the twelve surviving chapters of Book V concerning the last stages of the revolt there is only a brief and indirect reference to *libertas* in the short battle speech of Civilis.[2] So the ideology of the revolt is dominated by the theme of freedom, but this is presented much more delicately than in the *Agricola*.

The same can be said of Tacitus' treatment of the great rebellions in the *Annals*. The account of the Arminius war in *Annals* I and II follows the method of the *Histories*. A summary of a splendid speech by Arminius on the freedom theme in 1.59 is followed by the allusive *altercatio* between Arminius and his Quisling brother Flavus in 11.10. Then in 11.15 the summary of a battle speech of Arminius concludes with the familiar theme in masterly compression: ' meminissent modo avaritiae crudelitatis superbiae; aliud sibi reliquum quam tenere libertatem aut mori ante servitutem?'[3] In the second hexad of the *Annals* the story of the British war is enlivened by the summary of a speech of Caratacus about freedom, and the novelty of his speech to Claudius at Rome, which depicts the dignified behaviour of a barbarian in adversity.[4] The great revolt of Boudicca in Book XIV is interpreted by three assertions of the *libertas* theme. First the detailed account of the maltreatment of Boudicca leads to the resolution of the Iceni and Trinovantes to recover their freedom and destroy the Roman colony of Camulodunum, *arx aeternae dominationis*.[5] Then a powerful set speech of

---

[1] *Ibid.* 69.      [2] *Hist.* 5.17.2.

[3] ' Let them think only of Roman greed, cruelty and pride; what else have they left but to keep their freedom or to die before they are enslaved?"

[4] *Ann.* 12.34, 37.      [5] *Ibid.* 14.31.

Boudicca is summarized.[1] Finally the arrival of Polyclitus gives an opportunity to present the scorn of free barbarians for enfranchized slaves.[2]

So Tacitus in his three historical works presents a remarkable series of variations on the theme of the barbarian as *vindex libertatis*, using historical material, but developing it with all the skill of the rhetorical schools. Comparison with Caesar is instructive. In either case the barbarians were indeed fighting for the defence of freedom. Caesar was well aware of this, occasionally underlined it briefly, and once developed the theme in a striking speech.[3] The theme is there but it does not dominate or deflect the narrative. But Tacitus is engrossed by the theme, and by the presentation of the events, to the detriment of the portrayal of the barbarians themselves, especially in the *Annals*. He touches in the barbarian background with details that have become traditional. The account of the Druids at the taking of Mona is conventional stuff. There is a very compressed reference to human sacrifice and divination in groves described as *sacris superstitionibus saevi*, and there is a troop of frenzied females dressed like Furies.[4] The massacre of Romans at Verulamium is duly accomplished with attendant horrors, summarized as *caedes patibula ignes cruces*.[5] There are passing sneers at barbarians *laeti praeda et laborum segnes* and to 'sonores barbarorum et inanes minas'.[6] But in all this Tacitus is not expressing an *opinion* about the barbarians. He is writing literary history according to the common-place book. His opinion or his admiration comes out unexpectedly in the

---

[1] *Ibid.* 14.35.   [2] *Ibid.* 14.39.2–3.
[3] Above p. 24.   [4] *Ann.* 14.30.1–3.
[5] *Ibid.* 14.33.6.
[6] *Ibid.* 14.33.4, 36.1. 'Delighting in booty and reluctant to toil.' 'The noise and empty threats of a barbarian host.'

sentence that conjoins the suicide of Boudicca with that of the disobedient *praefectus castrorum* of the second legion.[1] This should be taken with the portrayal of Caratacus in defeat and the tribute to Arminius at the end of Book II. Tacitus in the *Annals* positively and explicitly admires the barbarian leaders. This is a new attitude, even if foreshadowed by the implications of Caesar's treatment of Vercingetorix. Tacitus may not admire the barbarians *en masse*, but he does not go out of his way to underline their more horrid characteristics. Even in the description of the scene of the Varus disaster the unpleasant behaviour of the victors is barely pencilled in. ' Quot patibula captivis, quae scrobes, utque signis et aquilis per superbiam inluserit.'[2] That is only a bow to the conventions, very different from the reaction of Velleius.

There are a number of lesser episodes in the *Annals* concerned with the barbarian resistance which show a rather different attitude. When Tacitus describes the despatch of Italicus, a half-Romanized prince of the Cherusci who had been educated in Italy, to take over the leadership of his people, the consequent civil war between sections of the Cherusci is represented in now familiar colours as a choice between *libertas* and *servitus*.[3] Tacitus is not very interested in the Romanization of Italicus, pausing only to remark that his personal military equipment was half Roman, half Germanic.[4] But he does observe that Italicus gained popularity among the Cherusci by his addiction to certain vices: ' vinolentiam ac libidines, grata barbaris usurpans '.[5]

[1] *Ibid.* 14.37.6.
[2] *Ibid.* 1.61. ' What forms of torture they devised for their prisoners, and how insolently Arminius mocked the Roman standards.'
[3] *Ibid.* 11.16–17.
[4] *Ibid.* 11.16.2.
[5] *Ibid.* 11.16.4. ' Given to drunkenness and lust, to the delight of his barbarian subjects.'

The *Germania* prepares us for the drunkenness, but leaves us astonished at the addition of the second term. For the author of the Germania, freedom from *libidines* was the great virtue of the Germanic tribes. This casual phrase is plain misrepresentation, and characteristic of the scornful attitude towards Italicus that marks the whole passage, which dismisses him with the final remark, ' per laeta per adversa (Italicus) res Cheruscas adflictabat ': he was a disaster to the Cherusci in success and misfortune alike.

Another barbarian whom Tacitus does not admire is Gannascus, a kind of ex-Quisling, who stirred up the Germanic Chauci in the time of Claudius.[1] The great legate Corbulo got rid of this Gannascus, but not by honest fighting. Tacitus comments: ' nec . . . degeneres insidiae fuere adversus transfugam et violatorem fidei '.[2] Gannascus had formerly served in the Roman auxiliary army, and later changed sides. That sufficed to prevent Tacitus from investing him with the glamour of an Arminius. One may contrast Tacitus' handling of Boiocalus, leader of the obscure Ampsivarii.[3] This man also had served in the Roman auxiliaries, and for fifty years had supported the Romans in tribal politics. So when his tribe was refused the grant of certain vacant lands by the legate of the lower Rhine army, Boiocalus made an impassioned speech about the proper treatment of loyal friends and left the scene with a famous *mot*: ' deesse nobis terra . . . in qua moriamur non potest '.[4] These three episodes taken together may reveal the private opinion of Tacitus as a Roman senator—mostly concealed in the rest of

[1] *Ibid.* 11.18.1.
[2] *Ibid.* 11.19.4. ' Trickery was not ignoble against a turncoat and a traitor.'
[3] *Ibid.* 13.55–56.
[4] *Ibid.* 13.56.3. ' There can be no shortage of land to die in.'

the *Annals*—that barbarians were only admirable when they were on your side, and not always even then.

It is a short step to the attitude of Tacitus in the *Histories*. He cannot be said openly to admire the Batavian Civilis as he admired Arminius. There is not much characterization of the man beyond the initial tribute, 'ultra quam barbaris solitum ingenio sollers', and later a passing reference to his *saevitia ingenii*.[1] A certain cunning appears in his actions, and a conscious self-interest, as in his refusal to commit himself formally to the Gallic cause, and in his persistent attempt to cover his rebellion by the pretence of supporting Vespasian. Twice Tacitus goes out of his way to cast discredit on Civilis. First there is the account of Civilis cutting his long hair in fulfilment of a barbarian vow, after the slaughter of the Roman legions.[2] This is followed by the report that Civilis let his young son execute prisoners for amusement. Later there occurs the story of Civilis fitting out a war fleet on the lower Rhine to intercept Roman supplies coming from Gaul.[3] Tacitus makes an odd comment on this sensible plan of Civilis, that the fitting out of the fleet was due to the native *vanitas* of his race. Tacitus is by no means uncritical of this *vindex libertatis*, whom he suspects of seeking a private empire. But the last surviving chapter of the *Histories* provides a compliment of sorts.[4] Civilis, betrayed by his fellows, seeks a colloquy with the Romans. He is weary of his troubles and moved by that desire for survival which commonly corrupts heroes: 'etiam spe vitae quae plerumque magnos animos infringit'. Civilis was no

---

[1] *Hist.* 4.13.2. 'He had a natural cleverness unusual in barbarians.' Cf. 4.23.3, 'nec ulla ipsis sollertia'. For *saevitia*, 4.63.1.

[2] *Ibid.* 4.61.1.

[3] *Ibid.* 5.23.2.

[4] *Ibid.* 5.26.1.

Boudicca, and Tacitus admired him the less. The consequence is a more realistic portrayal of the barbarians.

Though there is some conventional material in the *Histories*—the presence of barbarian women on the battlefield, the mention of Druids and their prophecies[1]—there are some details of barbarian practices, which are not documented in earlier sources. Such are the tossing of the war-leader Brinnus from a shield, *more gentis*, and the bringing out of the totem poles from the sacred groves for battle.[2] This was mentioned in the *Germania*, but less accurately. Tacitus also stresses the role of the Germanic prophetess Veleda in the uprising. He notes her isolation from human contact, and underlines the peculiar attitude of the Germans to such personalities: ' augescente superstitione arbitrantur deas '.[3] The description is fuller than in a similar passage of the *Germania* where the author in an ambiguous phrase seems to be denying that the Germans regarded their prophetesses as divine.[4] But perhaps the most critical remark that Tacitus makes about the Germans is that attributed to the Gaul Tutor: ' Germanos ... non iuberi non regi sed cuncta ex libidine a gere '. This recalls a similar comment in the *Annals* about the Frisii: ' nationem illam regebant in quantum Germani regnantur'.[5] The thought is not quite original, since Caesar said something like it. But it is out of line with what the *Germania* had to say about the Germanic tribal councils.[6] So in the *Histories* Tacitus shows more detachment and

---

[1] *Ibid.* 4.18.3, 54.2.

[2] *Ibid.* 4.15.2, 22.2. *Germ.* 7.3.

[3] *Hist.* 4.61.2. ' With increasing credulity they think of them as divine.'

[4] *Germ.* 8.3.

[5] *Hist.* 4.76.2, *Ann.* 13.54.2. ' Germans accept no orders or rules, but act just as they please.' Cf. Caesar, *B.G.* IV.1.9, cited p. 21 n. 1.

[6] *Germ.* 11, 22.3–4.

originality than elsewhere. A more critical portrait is the result. The German appears as an untrustworthy, undisciplined character, capable of occasional savagery and other behaviour abhorrent to a civilized man. But there is no strong feeling of disapproval, even in these contexts, much less so than in the adverse passages of the *Germania*.

So far as his historical works survive it is only in the *Agricola* that Tacitus stops to give a formal account of a barbarian people. He may have done so again for the Britanni in the missing Claudian books of the *Annals*, but he does not do so for the Germans or the Parthians in the early books of the *Annals* or the *Histories*. The fact is itself significant. The Romans were becoming used to their barbarians, and only the latest novelty called for detailed comment. The ethnology of the Britons in the *Agricola* is brief and sketchy, though he claims to be giving the first well-documented account of the whole country. He devotes a chapter and a half, some forty-four lines, to geography and products, and another chapter to the racial origins of the Britons in terms of physique, language and religion.[1] *Mores* and *instituta* as such receive a bare twelve lines, mostly about political leadership and warfare.[2] Tacitus comments also on the *ferocia* and relative docility of the Britons, connecting these qualities with the theme of *libertas* and *servitus*.[3] Everything else is dismissed with the easy formula: ' ceteri manent quales Galli fuerunt '.[4] It is all very summary, but enough to show that he had the same racial classification in mind as the author of the *Germania*, based on physique, language, and social

---

[1] *Agric.* 10, 12.3–7, and 11.
[2] *Ibid.* 12.1–3, 13.1.
[3] *Ibid.* 11.5, 13.1.
[4] *Ibid.* 11.5. ' For the rest they are still as the Gauls once were.'

organization. As for physique, he picks out salient characteristics—size of limbs, type of hair and complexion. There is
little evaluation, except for the qualities associated with
*libertas*. But there is a touch of contempt in the reference to
religious practices, summarized as *superstitionum per-
suasiones*.[1] Tacitus dislikes the native *audacia*, which is not
sustained in adversity.[2] This recalls Caesar and Strabo on the
Gauls.

Tacitus has nothing to say directly about the intellectual
abilities of the Britons, except for a scornful aside ' ut inter
barbaros parum compertum '—being barbarians, they lack
information.[3] No Briton is commended like the Chatti and
Civilis for *sollertia*. Elsewhere, in the famous chapter about
the civilizing of Britain, there is a compressed summary of
the people as previously *dispersi ac rudes*.[4] There follows the
description of the popularity of Latin literary education and
Italian material culture among the upper classes. Here the
term *imperiti* makes its reappearance: ' id . . . apud imperitos
humanitas vocabatur '. The implication is, as in Caesar's
*homines imperiti ac barbari*, that the Britons are men new to
the ways of civilization. But Tacitus is not interested in the
rudeness of the Britons as such. His target is still the theme of
*libertas* and the consequences of *servitus*. So once more
Tacitus' obsession with *libertas* obscures his reaction to
barbarians in themselves. He admires them insofar as they
try to maintain their dignity whether as independent or as
subject peoples. But between the lines one may read that
Tacitus' attitude to barbarian life was decidedly superior.

A few passing references touch on other unpleasing
characteristics, the *saevitia* of Boudicca, and the *adrogantia* of

[1] *Ibid.* 11.4. ' Accepted beliefs.'       [2] *Ibid.*
[3] *Ibid.* 11.1.       [4] *Ibid.* 21.1. ' Scattered and lacking culture.'

the Caledonians in not admitting defeat: ' nihil ex adrogantia remittere '.[1] The phrase is surprising because he normally admires those who fight for liberty, and *adrogantia* was the quality that Caesar found most objectionable in Ariovistus. In a colourful account of the despair of the conquered Caledonians Tacitus adds an ambivalent detail: 'satis... constabat saevisse quosdam in coniuges et liberos tamquam misererentur '. The choice of the disapproving word *saevisse* is deliberate.[2] Tacitus, like Strabo, is shocked at this sort of behaviour. Altogether Tacitus has nothing good to say about the Britons outside the context of *libertas*. His obsession with this is an irrelevant intrusion of the politics of senatorial society into an alien sphere. Tacitus himself indicated that the pacified Britons readily adopted the Roman civilization, the *delenimenta vitiorum*, and lost the zest for adventurous living in the cause of liberty.[3] Strip off the literary camouflage of *libertas*, and you find in all three of Tacitus' books the traditional dislike and distrust of the barbarians or of certain of their characteristics, which is the kernel of what we now call race hatred. This distrust did not develop into a big thing because men like Tacitus were after all conscious of being on the winning side. Britannia like Gallia was *domita* in terms of peace and war alike.

There is a possibility that this dislike or distrust had certain practical consequences. The adoption of the Roman civilization by the aristocracy of the northern Gauls and Britain is well documented in many minute particulars known both from literature and archaeology. It receives official

---

[1] *Ibid.* 16.1, 27.3.
[2] *Ibid.* 38.2. ' It is a fact that some of them savaged their wives and children apparently out of pity.'
[3] *Ibid.* 21.3.

recognition in the speech of Claudius recorded in a long inscription from Lugdunum, and in three set treatments by Tacitus, who was a consular senator. These are his own version of the Claudian speech in the *Annals*, the *Agricola* passage just mentioned, and the great speech of the legate Cerialis to the assembly of the northern Gauls in the *Histories*.[1] In each of these documents the theme is that the adoption of Roman culture by the Celtic aristocracy opened the door to service in the Roman state, eventually at the highest level. In the *Annals*, as in the actual speech of Claudius, the once trousered Gauls become togaed senators. In the *Histories* the Gauls themselves rule provinces and command legions. In the *Agricola* one reads that at a lower level *honoris aemulatio pro necessitate fuit*. The words are concise but not obscure. ' Ambition for office (i.e. in the Roman army) made compulsion unnecessary.'

But did it work out quite as indicated? Professor Syme, in a notable chapter of his *Tacitus*, has observed a peculiar thing about the role of Gauls in the service of Rome.[2] It is not that they do not appear, but that having put in an appearance, they disappear. In every other zone of the Roman empire, even in the eastern Greek-speaking provinces, there is a clear and regular pattern in the recruitment of local aristocrats to the Roman public service. First the Roman citizenship is secured in the early Principate when it was still comparatively unusual—' rarum nec nisi virtuti pretium '.[3] The next generation secures equestrian status appropriate to the family's wealth, leading to service in the commissioned posts of the Roman army, and to procuratorships in the imperial adminis-

---

[1] Dessau, *I.L.S.* 212; Tac. *Ann.* 11.24–25.1, *Hist.* 4.74.1, 4.
[2] R. Syme, *Tacitus*, i.461–2.
[3] Tac. *Ann.* 3.40.1–2.

tration. Finally the sons of successful procurators become senators. This is a familiar tale in this prosopographical age, everywhere except in northern Gaul and Britain. Despite the encouragement of the emperor Claudius, senators do not emerge from northern Gaul in the following century except for rare and widely separated instances. At the procuratorial level one may consult the lists and statistics compiled by the learned Professor Pflaum for the later second and early third centuries, the period when inscriptions are most abundant.[1] The origins of nearly a hundred equestrian procurators are known in this period. They come from all over the empire, and are evenly distributed over nearly all the provinces, large and small alike, in Europe, Africa and Asia Minor, with the great exception of the three northern Gauls, Rhaetia, and Britain, the lands of the Celtic and Germanic peoples. Even the Balkan provinces, which culturally were far behind the three Gauls, have their representatives. But northern Gaul and its affiliated lands present a blank, in striking contrast to the southern province of Gallia Narbonensis, which has a steady quota of procurators and senators. There is an exception of the kind that tests the rule. The old veteran settlement of *colonia Agrippinensis* in the Rhineland produces a single procurator.[2] It may be that procurators of north Gallic origin will appear in new documents or lurk undetected in the sixteen men of uncertain origin listed by Pflaum. But even so the contrast is remarkable. The only western provinces otherwise unattested on the roll of equestrian procurators are the small and remote regions of Lusitania and Mauretania Tingitana.

Yet equestrian promotion did not present the same diffi-

---

[1] H. G. Pflaum, *Les procurateurs équestres* (Paris, 1950), 183 f., 186, 190 f.
[2] *I.L.S.* 1372, C. Titius Similis.

culty to a provincial as did admission to the Senate. It was entirely in the hands of the emperor, and was not subject to the prejudices of the narrow electoral body of jealous senators which controlled two-thirds of the annual admissions to the Roman senate. If the northern Gauls did not become equestrian officials, it must be either because they were unambitious or because the emperors did not want them. Neither supposition is true for the first half of the first century A.D. Apart from incidental sources, Tacitus in the *Histories* and *Annals* documents the ready admission of the Gallic nobility to the *militia equestris*. In his account of the rebellion of A.D. 69 Tacitus names six Gallic leaders, excluding the Germanic Batavians. Four of these six were serving officers of the regular forces of the Roman army as *praefecti cohortis* or *praefecti alae*.[1] Tacitus also mentions a certain Julius Calenus who was a legionary military tribune,[2] and refers to a group of legionary centurions and tribunes of north Gallic origin.[3] In the *Annals* Tacitus recounts the part played by the Trevir Julius Indus as an officer of the regular army in putting down the rebellion of his fellow Trevir Julius Florus. This same Julius Indus celebrated the occasion by giving his daughter the name of Pacata or ' Pacified ', and marrying her off to another north Gallic equestrian, Julius

---

[1] The two not designated as officers are Julius Sabinus and Julius Valentinus (*Hist.* 4.55.2, 68.4, 70.5). Julius Tutor was set for a distinguished career: ' ripae Rheni a Vitellio praefectus ' (*Ibid.* 4.55.2). Julius Classicus, of the old nobility, was *praefectus alae Trevirorum* (*Ibid.* 2.14.1, 4.55.1). Alpinius Montanus was *praefectus cohortis* (*Ibid.* 3.35.2, 4.31.1, 5.19.3). Julius Briganticus, a Batavian on his mother's side, was *praefectus alae singularium* (*Ibid.* 2.22.3, 4.70.2). Claudius Labeo, a Batavian officer, was an active pro-Roman (*Ibid.* 4.18.4, 56.3, 66); otherwise the Batavian *principes* serving as officers in their native units solidly supported the rising.

[2] *Hist.* 3.35.2.

[3] *Ibid.* 4.61.3.

Alpinus Classicianus, who later appears as a career procurator under Nero.[1]

It is generally true that in the Principate as a whole, military tribunes of north Gallic origin are extremely scarce.[2] But in this short period of a generation, which Tacitus illuminates—briefly but intensely—at two widely separated moments, it is apparent that down to A.D. 69 the admission of Gallic gentry to the Roman administrative class was proceeding normally. Tacitus documents the loyalty to Rome of Gallic nobles such as the Trevir Indus in the rebellion of A.D. 20, and Julius Auspex of the Remi,[3] the man who turned the tide in favour of Rome at the critical assembly of A.D. 70. Tacitus himself writes in favour of the promotion of Gauls to legionary legateships and provincial governorships in the speech of Cerialis to which he devotes so much space and talent. This final stage had actually begun with the career of the Aquitanian Julius Vindex, the governor of Lugdunensis who conspired with Galba against Nero.[4]

What then went wrong? Not only are Gallic gentry missing from the upper cadres of the administration, but Professor Syme has shown how rare it was for Gallic peasantry to be recruited into the serving ranks of the legionary army, as distinct from the auxiliary service.[5] The northern Gauls had shown the necessary ambition at the time of the request of the Aedui to Claudius for admission to the senatorial order.[6] There was no bar against southern Gauls from Narbonensis, which like southern Spain and later Africa secures more than

---

[1] Tac. *Ann.* 3.42. *Année épigraphique*, 1936 n. 3.
[2] Syme, *Tacitus*, i.456 n. 5.
[3] Tac. *Hist.* 4.69.1. Cf. Claudius Labeo, above p. 54, n. 1.
[4] Syme *op. cit.* i.461–2, and 462 n. 2 for other possibilities.
[5] *Ibid.* i.456 n. 4.
[6] Tac. *Ann.* 11.25.1.

its quota of *boni viri et locupletes* in the upper levels of the Roman administration.[1]

The simplest answer would be that the occurrence of three considerable revolts in north Gaul within forty years, two of which came in quick succession in the years 68 and 70, was too much for the central government to stomach.[2] The last at any rate was dressed up as a positive breakaway movement aimed at founding an *imperium Galliarum*, even if the first two, as is commonly held nowadays, were motivated only by the harshness and exactions of the provincial governors.[3] The Gauls were found wanting in the basic virtue of *obsequium*, respectful collaboration, on which the working of the administration depended.[4] So henceforth they were rejected as candidates for promotion in the public services, and their common people who had fully supported the rebellions were excluded from the vital core of the Roman army. This explanation is doubtless part of the answer, and it would do very well if it were not altogether contrary to the pragmatism of Roman policy. One expects to find at least those who had been loyal to the Roman cause securing a political reward. But the descendants of Indus and Auspex were excluded, it seems, as effectively as those of the secessionists Classicus and Tutor from high Roman office.

There must be some factor apart from the question of loyalty operating to the disadvantage of northerners, some factor which did not operate in southern Gaul, and which worked with cumulative effect. Even the south had been involved in the events of A.D. 68, when Vienna supported the

---

[1] Syme, *op. cit.* ii.589 f.

[2] Cf. Syme similarly, *op. cit.* i.463.

[3] Cf. P. A. Brunt, *Latomus* 1959, 531 f., following Dio (63.22.1a), and Tacitus (*Ann.* 3.40).

[4] Cf. Syme *op. cit.* i.28, for *obsequium*.

doubtful cause of Vindex, and was ranged against the Roman colony of Lugdunum.[1] There remains only the marked difference of culture between the heavily Romanized south and the still largely barbarian and occasionally barbaric north, the region which still differed greatly in *sermo*, *mores* and *instituta* from Latinized Narbonensis. There are certain negative implications in the elder Pliny's description of Gallia Narbonensis. He gives it a famous accolade as 'agrorum cultu, virorum morumque dignatione, amplitudine opum nulli provinciarum postferenda, breviterque Italia magis quam provincia '.[2] Now the three northern provinces by the time of Pliny surpassed Narbonensis in scale of landed wealth —*agrorum cultus* and *amplitudo opum*. But they fell short in the vital thing, *virorum dignatio*. The phrase in its implied contrast sums up all those defects of custom and character delineated and underlined by Caesar, Strabo and Tacitus, from which the southerners had been purged. This is not colour bar, but it is certainly racial or cultural prejudice.

There is, however, a touch of something akin to colour bar. The Roman witnesses are allergic not to the complexions of the northern European, but to his vast and beastly size, his *immania corpora* and *latos artus*. The author of the *Germania* comments on the sordid conditions by which the Germans grew up ' in hos artus haec corpora quae miramur '.[3] Tacitus comments in the *Annals* on the huge limbs of the men of Arminius, and in the *Agricola* the size of the Caledonians reminds him of the Germans.[4] This all goes back to Caesar

---

[1] Tac. *Hist.* 1.65.

[2] Pliny, *Nat. Hist.* 3.31. ' In cultivation of its land, in the worth of its men and manners, in scale of wealth, second to no other province: briefly, another Italy.' Cf. *ibid.* 3.31 for differentiation by *sacra* and *lingua*.

[3] Tac. *Germ.* 20.1.

[4] *Ann.* 1.64, 2.14, 21. *Agric.* 11.2.

who recorded the panic caused in his army by the *ingens magnitudo corporum* of the men of Ariovistus.[1] He himself used a strong term for the physique of the Suebic Germans: 'immani corporum magnitudine'. But the most revealing comment on size comes in an anecdote of Caesar about the Belgic Atuatuci making fun of the tiny Romans. He adds that 'practically all the Gauls despise our lack of height compared to their own stature'.[2] Livy gives the classical illustration of this theme in his description of a champion fight between a Celtic giant and a diminutive Roman.[3] The Gaul, as handsome as he is huge, gaily dressed and decked with gilded weapons, utters battle cries and performs a war-dance in front of his small, silent, unadorned and well-trained adversary. He looms over his opponent as a *moles superne imminens*. All in vain, of course. Two thrusts of the Roman's utilitarian sword finish him off, and he falls Homerically to cover a great deal of ground. After the discovery of the Germans and Britons this physical prejudice, which even Caesar felt resentfully, was transferred to them. Strabo records carefully the atrocious size of the Britons. They were bigger than the Gauls, and half a foot taller than the average Roman, and he notes that the Germans differed from the Gauls in their excessive size.[4] But however vast the Germans were, it was the Celts of Gaul and Britain who were provincial subjects of Rome. Their physique, if less tremendous than the German, was still bad enough to act as a perpetual minor irritant with all the other things that the Romans disliked in them.

These minor irritants included trousers, the Celtic *braca*. The Romans were the people of the toga, and they had the

---

[1] Caesar, *B.G.* I.39.1.  
[3] Livy 7.9.8–10, 12.  
[2] *Ibid.* II.30.4, IV.1.9.  
[4] Strabo 4.5.2 (200).

same curious contempt for the *braca* that certain classes of English people have for the Scots kilt.[1] Cicero exploits this in his sneer at the consular Piso, whose family had connections with the ancient Roman colony of Placentia in Cisalpine Gaul. That enabled Cicero to call him 'a disgrace to his trousered kinsmen'—*bracatae cognationis dedecus*. So too in his defence of a proconsul of southern Gaul he jeers at the provincial witnesses as 'giants in trousers'.[2] The familiar lampoon against Caesar's new senators, supposedly from Gaul, has the same gibe: 'They have taken off their trousers and donned the purple stripe.'[3] Strabo knew the point at issue when he described the Romanized natives of southern Spain and Gaul as τογᾶτοι, people of the toga.[4] So it is of interest that the elder Pliny says of southern Gaul that it was formerly called *Gallia bracata*, but is now known as *Gallia Narbonensis*, after its chief city Narbo.[5] The opprobrious epithet no longer applied. Akin to it was the designation of north Gaul as *comata*, the land of the long-haired people. Strabo connected long hair and trousers in his account of Celtic differentia.[6] Tacitus uses the term with a clear innuendo when he introduces the Gallic notables, who address the famous petition to Claudius for senatorial status, as the *primores Galliae quae comata appellatur*—the leaders of long-haired Gaul—a term which he uses nowhere else in his many references to Gaul.[7]

The debate about the Gallic petition in the *Annals* contain

---

[1] A reminiscence from my observations during the 1939–45 war.
[2] Cicero, *In Pisonem*, 53. *pro Fonteio*, 33. Cf. above p. 17.
[3] Suetonius, *Julius*, 80.2.
[4] Strabo 3.2.15 (151). Cf. 4.1.12 (186).
[5] Pliny, *Nat. Hist.* 3.31. He uses *comata* for the north, *ibid.* 4.105.
[6] Strabo 4.4.3 (196).
[7] Tac. *Ann.* 11.23.1.

E 2

a remarkable example of the sustained use of racial arguments against the equal treatment of foreign peoples. The opponents of the proposal held that the Senate should be recruited from native Italians and kindred peoples, *indigenae, consanguinei*, and objected to the admission of hordes of *alienigenae*.[1] In Tacitus' version, much more clearly than in the original speech, Claudius meets the argument in its own terms, insisting on the advantage of racial mixture as demonstrated by history.[2] This evidence should not be pressed too far, because it comes from a highly rhetorical context. But still it shows where the prejudices that I have been exploring could lead. The emperor meets his opponents half way when he says that the Gallic nobility were ' iam moribus artibus adfinitatibus nostris mixti '. They are all right, they no longer wear trousers. The negative implication is also clear: ' if they remain isolated in their Celtic environment we won't let them into our order '. That apparently is just what happened.

One returns to the conclusion already foreshadowed by the speech of Critognatus in the *Bellum Gallicum* and indicated by Strabo. Racial prejudice against the northern barbarians existed in the Roman mind over a long period of time, and could focus on details of character, physique and customs. It could be brought to a head if there arose a clash of interests within a small community. But the occasion for this did not arise except within the artificial framework of the Roman administrative machine. The force of such racial feeling as existed was ever being undermined by the non-exclusiveness of cultures. A strong repulsion could not develop when one of the two peoples concerned was so anxious to adopt the customs of the other. The minor irritants that brew the deadly potion were ever losing their

[1] *Ibid.* 11.23.3–4.      [2] *Ibid.* 11.24.

strength. But only in Narbonensis were settlements of Celts and Romans involved together through Italian colonization in a large-scale experiment of contiguous living. Here the Gallic life simply faded away. In the northern zone of the three Gauls and Britain, which was more resistant to change, distance and the lack of extensive foreign settlement prevented the development of a racial crisis, but the same factors tended to exclude the leading men from the service and honours of the Roman state. Otherwise racial prejudice appears simply as a latent and harmless attitude of mind that manifested itself in literary men when they occasionally turned their attention to the peripheries of the empire. An illustration of the mildness of the sentiment can be found in that most typical of educated Romans of the period, the younger Pliny, a man who had never visited any European province. A southern Gaul from Vienna, appearing before the tribunal of the emperor at Rome, dispensed with an advocate and conducted his own defence. Pliny commented in mild surprise at this Celtic portent: ' tamquam homo Romanus et bonus civis in negotio suo mature et graviter loquebatur '.[1] Pliny did not quite expect it any more than he expected to find bookshops at Lugdunum.[2] But he certainly approved.

[1] Pliny, *Epp.* 4.22.2. ' He spoke in his own case effectively and weightily like a man of Rome and a sound citizen.'
[2] *Ibid.* 9.11.2.

# 3

# STRIFE AND RIVALRY WITHIN THE EMPIRE

## Romans and Greeks

Romans were very conscious of their immense debt to Greek thought and letters, and they took for granted the coexistence in the empire of the two cultures summed up in the common phrase *uterque sermo noster*—' our two languages '. But there is surprisingly little information about what Romans thought of their Greek contemporaries at any particular moment.[1] There is much more known about the reverse relationship: Strabo, Plutarch, and Lucian in their different periods reveal a great deal of what Greeks thought of the Roman world.[2]

---

[1] T. J. Haárhof, *The Stranger at the Gate*[2] (Oxford, 1948), concerned himself with this theme in the Republican period. Later B. Hardinghaus, *Tacitus und das Griechentum* (Diss. Munster, 1952), is the chief synoptic study. Not much can be made of the Augustan period, despite Livy's carping remarks about Alexander; cf. G. W. Bowersock, *Augustus and the Greek World* (Oxford, 1965), 109. For *uterque sermo* cf. Suet. *Claudius* 42.1.

[2] A considerable literature has grown around this second theme. The title of K. Fuchs' book, *Der geistige Widerstand gegen Rom in der antiken Weld* (Berlin, 1938), is characteristic of much modern discussion, which is often mistaken or exaggerated, in my opinion, in this sort of interpretation of the strains and irritations that arose naturally between rulers and ruled in a world where nationalism was virtually non-existent. J. Palm, *Rom, Römertum, und Imperium in der griechischen Literatur der Kaiserzeit* (Lunt, 1959), surveys the literary sources summarily, and has a useful bibliography. Cf. also Bowersock *op. cit.*, ch. X, and E. A. Baumann, *Beiträge zur Beurteilung der Römer in der antiken Literatur* (Diss. Rostock, 1930). J. H. Oliver, *The Ruling Power* (T.A. Ph. Soc., 1953), deals with the panegyrical attitude to Rome, in a commentary on Aristides' *Panegyricus*. For Lucian see also A. Peretti, *Luciano Uno Intellectuale Greco* (Firenze, 1946). Space prevented a discussion of Plutarch, especially his *De republica gubernanda*, or of Dio of Prusa, in my lecture. Jüthner (cited p. 1, n. 1) barely touches the theme in his chapter on Rome from either point of view.

But the Latin writers are apt to take the living Greek world for granted. The elder Pliny is not helpful, and there is no *Germania* for any Greek province of the empire. But there is Juvenal's famous outburst in the third Satire against the *urbs Graeca*, and there is Lucian's portrait of Roman society in his *Nigrinus* and his *De Mercede Conductis*, or ' Salaried Gentlemen '. These are two sides of the same coin, and much can be extracted from the comparison of them in detail. Finally, certain letters of Pliny illustrate contemporary attitudes towards Greeks in Roman society from the viewpoint of the boss class.

Lucian, in his two dialogues, has been taken by many scholars for an extreme exponent of culture prejudice and national animosity, perhaps too naively. Certainly he says a great many nasty things about Roman senators and their private lives. The two essays contain a formidable indictment of the society of Rome itself and of the ways of wealthy Romans. They are complementary. The *Nigrinus* deals with the whole pattern of life at the capital, while the *Salaried Gentlemen* describes the experiences of a Greek man of letters who seeks employment as a tutor of philosophy in the household of a Roman magnate. In the *Nigrinus* the main character is himself a Roman of moderate wealth and a student of philosophy. The essay contrasts life at Rome and life at contemporary Athens, to which Nigrinus intends to retire. Athens is a quiet university city where men live modestly, despising wealth, luxury and power, and practise a serious unpolitical life of social freedom and intellectual activity. Strangers who make a vulgar display of wealth are soon put in their place by the gentle mockery of the Athenians, and learn a better way of living.[1] But Rome is depicted as the

[1] *Nigrinus* 12–14.

modern Babylon. ' If you love pleasure, trickery, falsehood and banqueting, stay in Rome. Its streets are full of fornication, covetousness, perjury, delation, flattery, murder, false friendship and legacy hunting.' [1] Astonishing changes of fortune take place there. Slaves become masters, beggars turn into millionaires and princes. ' Men walk about stuffed with fantastic hopes.' [2] Lucian soon leaves these generalizations, and picks out specific detail. Overdressed men of great wealth, flaunting rings and purple robes, expect you to kneel before them and kiss their hands. They never greet you with a kiss in return, and think it a favour even to let you see their persons. [3] Their conceit is built up by throngs of flattering courtiers and dependants. Lucian notes that their real passion is not so much for wealth as for the envious admiration that wealth brings. [4] They live a life of topsy-turvy luxury in which only fantastic pleasures are valued—roses in midwinter and wines flavoured with spices. They deck themselves with garlands of flowers for their perfume, but wear them round their temples when they ought to hang them under their noses. Altogether Lucian reckons that the luxury of the Romans was based on a principle of solecism; they do everything the wrong way. [5]

He noted with particular dislike the Roman magnate's habit of using his servants in the streets to address other persons on his behalf, and to warn him of obstacles in his path. [6] ' If they use other peoples' eyes and voices, why don't they borrow their mouths to eat with? ' [7] Then there is the

---

[1] *Ibid.* 15–17. The longer citations of Lucian are compressed and paraphrased.

[2] *Ibid.* 20.                        [3] *Ibid.* 21.
[4] *Ibid.* 23.                        [5] *Ibid.* 31, 33.
[6] *Ibid.* 21.                        [7] *Ibid.* 34.

inordinate fuss that Romans make about wills and testaments.[1]
'The only true statement that a Roman makes in his whole
life is in his will', says Lucian. They continue with the same
folly after death, by means of instructions to their heirs for
funeral pyres, memorial services, and long inscriptions on
their tombs. Another folly of the living Roman was his
devotion to horse-races. 'The city is full of pictures of
jockeys and names of race-horses.[2] They talk about horses
at street corners. Horse-madness afflicts everyone, even
serious men.' This is part of a critical description of the crowds
and confusion that fill the baths and theatres of the great city.

So much for the *Nigrinus*. In itself it is no more than a
rather puritanical diatribe in the philosophical tradition
against the corruptions of the great city, realized in the
actualities of Rome. It is not only Romans, or wealthy
Romans, that Lucian lashes. When describing the crowds of
toadies fawning upon the wealthy he remarks: 'Even
philosophers do all this at Rome. Despite their beards and
mantles they behave worse than the rest, stuffing themselves
at banquets, and getting drunk openly. They are even prepared to sing.'[3] This leads him on to a short digression
criticizing philosophers who take salaries and 'put virtue up
for sale as in a shop'.[4] These unworthy philosophers are not
native Romans.

The central point in the satire is the vulgarity and lack of
taste of wealthy Romans. This Lucian cannot endure. It is the
same point that he made about the behaviour of wealthy
strangers at Athens. But those were not identified as Romans,
nor obviously intended for Romans. They are just any rich

[1] *Ibid.* 30.      [2] *Ibid.* 29.
[3] *Ibid.* 24–5.      [4] *Ibid.* 25.

young fools.[1] The only passage that is viciously anti-Roman
is the paragraph about wills and funeral rites. Lucian even
goes out of his way to suggest that the crowds of flattering
courtiers are mainly to blame for the beastliness of the
Romans. If less fuss were made about the wealth of the
wealthy they would soon mend their ways.[2] Besides, Lucian
puts his great sermon into the mouth of a philosopher who is
himself a Roman and a land-owner of Italy.[3] He is commended for his generosity and his indifference to his own
wealth, his modesty of life, and his spiritual teaching. The
force of the satire is increased by this setting: the best of the
Romans can no longer endure Rome. But this rather
diminishes the effect of the *Nigrinus* as a specimen of national
prejudice. It remains a satire on wealth rather than an attack
on the Romans for being Romans. But still it lays bare the
principle that bad feeling between people stems from their
differences of custom and behaviour. Lucian could forgive
the Romans their wealth but for their bad taste.

The *Salaried Gentlemen* develops a theme touched only
lightly in the *Nigrinus*: the reaction of the underdog to his
master. The essay is about an ambitious young man of
letters from the Greek east, who goes to Rome to make his
fortune as the protégé of a Roman magnate. Lucian draws a
skilful picture of such a man's entry into Roman society, his
rise, decline and final ruin. He starts by criticizing the
ambition itself. Such men pretend that they are driven to this
course by poverty, but it is the poverty of the middle classes.
Their true motive is the passion for luxury, to eat fine
dinners, ride in fine carriages, and have a fat salary into the

[1] *Ibid.* 13.
[2] *Ibid.* 23.
[3] *Ibid.* 26. The scene is set at Rome, *ibid.* 15, 17, 19.

bargain.[1] As he warms to his subject Lucian turns the heat of his satire on to the Roman patrons, their vanity, frivolity, vulgarity and meannesss. The unfortunate candidate for professorial status is put through an insolent interview, his references are checked, and his past life intimately investigated.[2] Finally he is invited to a great dinner party. This serves as a sort of final board examination.[3] Everyone watches the Greek stranger, unfamiliar with Roman conventions, committing gaffes. The long-established members of the household view him with open jealousy. 'Who is this in the best seats?' they ask. 'The doors of Rome are open only to Greeks. Why are *they* preferred to *us*?'[4] If he survives all this there is yet another interview to discuss the delicate question of salary. The poor Greek is properly fooled. 'I am sharing my whole life with you,' says the patron. 'You will have the usual presents at the great festivals. You are a modest man, I am sure you haven't come for the sake of lucre.'[5] An old family friend remarks that you are being received into the best house in Rome. 'Many men would pay for the privilege.' So the professor ends up with a very small salary.[6]

He soons finds out that his patron cares nothing for philosophy. He only wants to be known to have a philosopher in his household, complete with mantle and long beard, and so to pass for a philhellene.[7] 'Take away the Roman's wealth,' says Lucian, 'and he is just an insolent brute and a voluptuary.'[8] When the novelty has worn off, the patron prefers an Alexandrian dancing master to his philosopher,

---

[1] *De Mercede Conductis* 5–7 with 3.  [2] *Ibid.* 11–12.
[3] *Ibid.* 14, 15–16.  [4] *Ibid.* 17.
[5] *Ibid.* 19.  [6] *Ibid.* 20.
[7] *Ibid.* 25.  [8] *Ibid.*

who is relegated to the worst place at the dining table, and treated as a servant by the patron's wife.[1] The household slaves take their cue, and he leads a wretched life. If he travels with the family he shares a seat with the cook or the jester. He has to carry his lady's lapdog, which licks his beard or produces a litter in his cloak.[2] Sometimes his lady pretends to be a bluestocking, studying philosophy and writing poems. But if she invites him to give a lecture, she interrupts it to read a note from her lover.[3] Even if his patron has genuine literary interests the effect is excruciating for the Greek professor, who has to praise atrocious compositions and admire the worst solecisms. Or he may be called upon to display his own talents during a drinking bout.[4] Finally the professor is dismissed in favour of a younger man, on some fictitious charge of seducing a serving maid or making eyes at a favourite slave.[5] Even this is not the end. Rumours are spread about his evil ways to discredit him with the public, for fear that he might reveal all the secrets of the household in which he spent the best years of his life.[6]

The tone of the narrative is decidedly hostile, more so than that of the *Nigrinus*. The Roman patron appears revolting. But there are certain reservations to be made. This essay was meant as a cautionary tale. 'That is what wealthy Romans can be like if you are greedy enough to take service in a private household.' One may dislike a class without hating the whole race. In the last phase of the tale, when the professor is finally ruined, Lucian remarks that the charges against him are believed because he is a Hellene, a man of easy virtue in Roman eyes, ready for any villainy. 'They

---

[1] *Ibid.* 26, 27.  
[2] *Ibid.* 33–4.  
[3] *Ibid.* 36.  
[4] *Ibid.* 35.  
[5] *Ibid.* 39–40.  
[6] *Ibid.* 41.

think this of us all,' Lucian continues, ' because many Hellenes come to their houses, with big beards and coarse cloaks, who practice the black arts, promising their patrons success in love affairs and spells to ruin their enemies. Knowing the servile tricks and greed of these types, they think we are all the same.'[1] Lucian is explaining and even justifying the Roman attitude. He began the essay by observing that most Greeks sought service at Rome for bad motives—the passion for an expense account—and he also pressed this criticism in the *Nigrinus*. This ability to see the situation from both sides gives peculiar value to his account. So too he understood the jealousy felt for the new Greek favourite by the older members of the household. He epitomizes the situation of the isolated Greek thus: ' You are only a foreigner wearing the pallium, and speaking Latin badly, among all those togaed Romans.'[2] He crystallizes the stresses and strains that developed when the representatives of the two cultures met in rivalry. This is perhaps more revealing than the general diatribe against the vulgarity and coarseness of the Roman millionaire. For Lucian in fact proves too much. There were on his own showing plenty of Greeks ready to put up with the vices and vulgarity. Lucian is voicing the protest only of a cultured minority.

But sometimes the protest goes deeper than the level of taste and good manners. There is a strange metaphor towards the end of the *Salaried Gentlemen*. He compares the wealthy Roman houses to fine books or scrolls, with golden bosses and purple bindings, much admired until you open them, but inside they are full of horrid stories, Thyestes devouring his children and Oedipus with his mother.[3] ' Open a well-dressed Roman and you will find a whole drama of Euripides.'

[1] *Ibid.* 40.  [2] *Ibid.* 24.

[3] *Ibid.* 41.

But this is not the main burden of the two essays. Generally the indictment is restricted to the themes of meanness and vulgarity. One is reminded of Mrs. Trollope flaying the Americans for their beastly habit of using spitoons. Much of the force of the satire is drawn from the elaboration of the discomfort of the life of the client at Rome when outside the palace of his patron, woken by a bell and rising at dawn, running round the crowded city, involved in fights at his lodgings, lying ill in bed from the after-effects of his grand dinners.[1] This is hardly the stuff of serious race-hatred.

Lucian was eventually hoist with his own petard. He himself took service, and had to explain this away in the short riposte known as the *Defence of Salaried Gentlemen* or *Pro Mercede Conductis*. He took service with the wealthiest of them all, the emperor, and his service consisted of a secretaryship in the office of the Prefect of Egypt. Lucian argues that this was the service of the State, and very different from service in a private house.[2] 'Those who are useful to cities and provinces differ from private servants as gold from lead.' His post is a 'big job', his salary comes 'from the Emperor', and consists of 'many talents, no miserable pittance'. The post will lead on to other promotions, even to a provincial governorship.[3] Besides, he adds, all the great officials of the empire are salaried. Even the emperor receives a salary, in the form of praise and worship in return for his help and forethought.[4] This is the common vocabulary of the panegyrists of Rome. Just so, but with much less restraint, do the cities of the empire express their gratitude to the Roman emperors in public addresses and inscriptions. Lucian was under no compulsion to speak like this. He had said

---

[1] *Ibid.* 24, 26, 30–1. *Nigrinus* 22.      [2] *Pro Mercede Conductis* 11.

[3] *Ibid.* 12.      [4] *Ibid.* 13.

nothing in his two essays to the detriment of the Roman administration. They are concerned only with Romans as private persons. He does not identify his magnates as senators or knights; Roman officials are mentioned only once in the *Nigrinus*, and to their credit, in a passage where Roman magistrates listening to the pleas of common men are contrasted with the idle mob-shunning rich.[1] However, Lucian's diatribes are not to be explained out of existence. They are very powerful, but they must be taken as a whole. The light is focussed on a tiny segment of Roman life. We feel how unpleasant the vulgarest of the Roman millionaires appeared to the exquisite creatures of the late Greek civilization, and how very nasty these could find the struggle to make good as professional men of letters at Rome.

Our *locus classicus* in Latin literature for the Roman dislike of Greeks is the passage of seventy lines in Juvenal's third satire.[2] It begins, ' I cannot endure a Rome that is full of Greeks '. This passage reproduces the picture we have seen in Lucian, but from the Roman side of the looking-glass. It is the Greek professional men that Juvenal dislikes, and he dislikes them because they are successful rivals of the home product for the favours of the great Roman patrons. They are a *gens divitibus nostris acceptissima*. Juvenal lists all the professions picked out by Lucian, and some others—men of letters,[3] doctors,[4] practitioners of black arts,[5] actors and musicians,[6] gymnasts and common entertainers, such as

---

[1] *Nigrinus* 34. The passage is slightly obscure.
[2] Juvenal, *Sat.* 3.58–125. Here I generally follow Friedlaender, who knew more about the history of manners than any other commentator. B. Hardinghaus discusses Juvenal in this context (*op. cit.* 72–74, p. 62, n. 1).
[3] *Grammaticus, rhetor, ibid.* 76–7.
[4] *Medicus, aliptes, ibid.* 76–7.
[5] *Augur, magus, ibid.* 77.
[6] *Tibicen, ibid.* 63. *Comoedus, ibid.* 93–4.

the tight-rope walker.[1] Characteristically the Roman-born Juvenal bothers least about those of most concern to Lucian, the philosophers. He does not list them in the main catalogue, and brings in philosophy only to enhance the enormity of the crime of one Celer, a professional Stoic who betrayed his patron.[2]

The burden of Juvenal's song is the reverse of Annie-get-your-gun. 'Anything I can do they can do better than me '—in Latin, 'non sumus ergo pares', and worse still: 'haec eadem licet et nobis laudare, sed illis creditur '.[3] Hence, 'there is no room for the sons of Rome where the Greek professor is in charge '. 'Non est Romano cuiquam locus hic ubi regnat Protogenes.' [4] By *hic* he means in the great houses of the Esquiline, for which the Greeks make as soon as they arrive, and where they become first the favourites and finally the bosses: 'viscera magnarum domuum dominique futuri '.[5] The Roman client can only exclaim ' me prior ille ... toro meliore recumbet?'[6] These are the very complaints that Lucian puts on the lips of his Roman rivals. Juvenal's prejudices are stirred especially by certain aspects of the Greek invasion. He most dislikes those who come from the distant Hellenistic provinces of Syria and Asia. Many lines are devoted to the horrid Syrians and their more horrid whores.[7] It is a Syrian who commits the worst crime of all, but the natives of old Hellas are almost as bad. Juvenal's jibe, ' quota portio faecis Achaei?'—' where is the old Greek

---

[1] *Schoenobates, ibid.* 77. *Gymnasia, ibid.* 115, cf. 67–8.

[2] *Ibid.* 115–16.

[3] *Ibid.* 92–3, 104. 'I too can flatter, but not so convincingly.'

[4] *Ibid.* 119–20.

[5] *Ibid.* 71–2.

[6] *Ibid.* 81–2. ' Is he to be given a better place than me?'

[7] *Ibid.* 62–6, 115–18.

scum?'—is hardly complimentary.[1] And the Greek who tried to fly was born in the very centre of Athens.[2]

Much space is given to Greek skill in flattery and simulation. It is a *gens adulandi prudentissima*. He gives examples that recur in Lucian: 'laudat sermonem indocti, faciem deformis amicae'.[3] The difference is that in Lucian the Greek finds himself forced to do this in a city that is already full of flatterers. In Juvenal he does it only too willingly. Juvenal lists their tricks in a long passage summed up as: 'semper, et omni nocte, potest aliena sumere vultum a facie'.[4] He believes all the charges that Lucian complained were falsely brought against the hapless Greek professor. Juvenal's version is that they will seduce your grandmother if there is no-one else available.[5] He ends with a curious inversion of the last misfortune of Lucian's man, finally ruined by a patron who feared that his protégé knew too much. In Juvenal the Greeks themselves try to ferret out the secrets of the house for an evil purpose: 'scire volunt secreta domus atque inde timeri'.[6] It is they too who drive out their Roman rivals with false rumours—'a drop of their native poison'—a fate reserved in Lucian for the Greek.[7]

Those lines assert the main theme: the jealousy felt by the native professional person for his too successful foreign rival. I remarked in my earlier lecture that the latent xenophobia

---

[1] *Ibid.* 61, 69–70.

[2] *Ibid.* 80.

[3] *Ibid.* 86–93. 'He praises the style of an uneducated friend and the beauty of a hideous mistress.' Cf. Lucian, *De Mercede Conductis* 35, above p. 68.

[4] Juvenal, *Sat.* 3, 100–8. 'At any time of night or day he can take his expression from another's face.'

[5] *Ibid.* 109–13.

[6] The line is commonly obelized as interrupting the sequence of thought in 108–15, but yet it is powerful and apposite.

[7] *Ibid.* 122–5.

felt for the northern barbarians did not come to a head for sheer lack of occasion. It needs pressure and rivalry to bring it to the boil. These emerged only once in the famous affair of Claudius' proposed admission of the *primores Galliae* to the Roman Senate.[1] Here in Juvenal and Lucian we find something similar, again within a narrow field, that of professional advancement under Roman patronage at Rome itself. The pressure manifests itself in an outburst of hostile feeling with clear overtones of cultural and national prejudice on both sides. But the question remains, how much genuine dislike is there in Juvenal for things Greek apart from the threat to his interests? The two attitudes are of course mixed up together. Juvenal's bitterest complaint is in a context of competition. The Greek will admit no rival, he is unwilling to share the booty.[2] Juvenal reckons this a national characteristic; ' gentis vitio . . . solus habet'. Their skill in flattery and dissimulation is summed up as ' natio . . . comoeda est'. The noun is insulting.[3] ' The *tribe* are born actors.'

But sometimes Juvenal expresses a dislike that is not motivated by fear or rivalry. Many Romans objected to the influence of Greek gymnastics and the *gymnicus agon* in Roman life, because of a supposed connection with homosexuality. Juvenal touches on this theme in a brief but effective allusion. ' Transi gymnasia atque audi facinus maioris abollae.' ' The crimes of the doctor's robe are worse than those of the singlet.'[4] Earlier he objected to the gymnasium in a sheerly xenophobic fashion: ' Rusticus ille tuus sumit trechedipna, Quirine, et ceromatico fert niceteria collo.'[5] The unusual agglomeration of Greek athletic termino-

---

[1] Above p. 60.    [2] Juvenal *op. cit.* 121–2.
[3] *Ibid.* 100.    [4] *Ibid.* 115.
[5] *Ibid.* 67–8. ' The Roman peasant dons his plimsols and wears his garland of victory on his oiled neck.'

logy in the company of Quirinus, the deified ancestor of
Rome, speaks for itself. So too Juvenal did not need to drag
in Syrian prostitutes and their turbans—' picta lupa barbara
mitra '.[1] Most of the section about the Syrians is irrelevant to
the rivalry theme which dominates the rest of the *urbs Graeca*
passage. In the Syrian section he is objecting to the infiltra-
tion into Roman life of Greek manners and culture—
' linguam et mores '—in any form.[2] Equally the ten lines
about the crimes of the Greeks, their seductions and their
murders, are purely abusive.[3] Juvenal is not objecting that
the Greeks were better than the Romans at these things. He
is just voicing plain prejudice, as he does more lightly in a
paragraph of the satire on women, where he complains that
ladies of fashion do and say everything in Greek: ' de Tusca
Graecula facta est, de Sulmonensi mera Cecropis, omnia
Graece, hoc sermone pavent . . . hoc cuncta effundunt animi
secreta ', etc.[4] This prejudice has a long paternity, stretching
back to the first Cato and his dislike of all things Greek.[5]

In the third satire Juvenal's dislikes and jealousies all fuse
together in the famous jibe: 'omnia novit Graeculus esuriens'.[6]
In this powerful *mot* the first two words summarize the main
complaint. ' These fellows are too clever by half,' just as they
are too ready with their tongues: ' Isaeo torrentior '.[7] Then
*esuriens*, the greedy Greek. This is not, as one might think,
a metaphor. Lucian devoted many paragraphs to the attrac-

---

[1] *Ibid.* 66.

[2] *Ibid.* 63.

[3] *Ibid.* 109 f.

[4] *Sat.* 6.185–96. 'The Tuscan lady turns Greek, a true daughter of
Cecrops, she talks and acts Greek only: she pours out the secrets of her heart
in Greek.'

[5] Cf. T. J. Haarhof, *The Stranger at the Gate*, 209 f.

[6] *Sat.* 3.77–8.

[7] *Ibid.* 74.

tions of the great Roman banquet.[1] These festivities were a
large part of the reward of the ambitious professional man.
Finally, that word *Graeculus*, used again in the essay on
women. The Latin diminutive is often contemptuous. Trajan
in a certain rescript to Pliny remarks: ' gymnasiis indulgent
Graeculi '. That may mean no more than ' our Greek friends
are devoted to their halls of exercise '. But when the same
Pliny in a satirical passage of his *Panegyric* refers to Domitian's
gymnastic festivals and brings in a *Graeculus magister*, the
tone is hostile. *Graeculus* is Latin for ' wog '.[2]

So in Juvenal there is an active if minor strain of national
and cultural prejudice at work. Certain letters of Pliny provide the correlate of all this. He is valuable because he alone
gives the point of view of just such a patron as Lucian and
Juvenal had in mind, though he is not so unpleasant or so
uneducated as Lucian makes his magnate out to be. Pliny had
the greatest admiration for the Greek men of letters who
frequented high society at Rome. Each of his first three
books contains the formal portrait of such a one. Euphrates
in Book I is a great Stoic teacher.[3] Pliny admires him as a
preacher rather than a thinker. The adjectives and adverbs
commend his style rather than his thought. ' Disputat sub-
tiliter graviter ornate...sermo est copiosus et varius.'[4] And,
just as in Lucian, Pliny admired his philosopher's get-up—
' proceritas corporis, decora facies '—and especially his great
white beard. When Pliny adds that his smooth tact—*comitas*
—equals his *sanctitas*, and that he attacks ' not men but vice ',

---

[1] Lucian, *Nigrinus* 22, 25, 33. *De Mercede Conductis* 15, 18, 26.

[2] Pliny, *Epp.* 10.40.2, *Pan.* 13.5.

[3] Pliny, *Epp.* 1.10. Cf. Hardinghaus, *Tacitus und das Griechentum*,
67–71 on Pliny.

[4] ' His argument is finely drawn, weighty and elaborate, while his style is
full and varied.'

we fear the worst. Euphrates was evidently a very smooth performer, and took care to gild the pill of virtue. This Euphrates was one of Juvenal's detested Syrians. So, too, was Artemidorus, another philosopher, but a tougher character than Euphrates.[1] Pliny notes the austerity of his life, and how he took no pleasure in eating and drinking. He adds that ' hardly one of those who call themselves philosophers nowadays could be compared to him '.[2] This calls to mind the strictures of Lucian.

Isaeus, Pliny's other Greek hero, was a professional orator, but a *scholasticus* or don, a lecturer and writer rather than a court advocate.[3] He specialized in extempore discourses, and gave public demonstrations of his skill, which Pliny greatly admired. Pliny regarded Isaeus also as a model of private virtue, though not at the level of the philosophers, and as free from the sharpness (*malitia*) of the court advocate. None of these three scholars seems to have lived in Pliny's household as salaried protégés, though he certainly gave a large sum of money to help Artemidorus when in special difficulties. Isaeus was presumably paid for his public discourses. The other two are described as personal friends of Pliny, and were men of high provincial status.[4]

Despite his respect for these men, it is apparent that Pliny had some reservations about *Graeculi* from the comparison that he makes between Artemidorus and the general run of such men and the fact that he could commend Euphrates for nothing more than *vitae sanctitas summa*. Elsewhere Pliny, reporting a session of Trajan's cabinet, commends the action of a civic magistrate of Vienna-on-Rhône, who had abolished a long-established gymnastic festival in the Greek style.[5]

---

[1] *Epp.* 3.11.     [2] *Ibid.* 6.     [3] *Ibid.* 2.3.
[4] *Ibid.* 1.10.8, 3.11.5.     [5] *Ibid.* 4.22.

Pliny remarked that such festivals had corrupted the habits of Rome, just as at Vienna, but the damage done at Rome was the greater because it set an example to the whole empire. The emperor Trajan and his cabinet agreed with Pliny's view of the Vienna affair. So when in the *Panegyric* Pliny jeered at the *Graeculus magister* of Domitian's Greek games he was expressing a widely held opinion. But it follows that you could be a philhellene like Pliny without approving of *gymnasia*.

In a well-known letter Pliny advises his friend Maximus, who is going out as an imperial commissioner to reorganize the ancient cities of classical Greece, in Achaea.[1] Pliny delivers a short panegyric of ancient Hellas—' illam veram et meram Graeciam '—the mother of civilization, liberty, and so forth. The terms of the panegyric go back to passages in Cicero, and may well constitute a commonplace of Latin oratory.[2] But Pliny continues that Maximus is to honour the Greeks for what they once were, and not to despise them because they have ceased to be like that: he is to maintain their *dignitas* and to respect even their boasts.[3] This is a more kindly version of Juvenal's ' true Greek scum '.[4] So Pliny the philhellene could find the same faults as the hostile and embittered Juvenal. He too recognized the *Graeculus esuriens*. But as a Roman senator his reaction was naturally very different. They were not competing with him for a job. Here we may wonder just what lurks behind Juvenal's bitterness. What job had he lost to a *Graeculus*? In the third satire

[1] *Ibid.* 8.24.

[2] Cicero, *pro Flacco* 61–2, *Ad Quint.* 1.1.6, 27–8. Cf. F. Zucker, *Philologus*, 84 (1928), 209 ff.

[3] Pliny, *Epp.* 8.24. 3, 5.

[4] Juvenal, *Sat.* 3.61.

he, like Lucian, talks only about private patronage. But there was a more profitable arena in which Greeks had been only too successful at the expense of ambitious Italians, that of the *militia equestris*, and promotion to the great imperial pro-curatorships. A most surprising feature of the period of Claudius and Nero is the high proportion of these posts that were held by provincials of Eastern Greek origin, at a time when *Graeculi*, unlike the Romanized gentry of the western provinces, were not able to secure admission to the senatorial order. At least a dozen such procurators can be found before the Flavian period—several of them being men of letters by origin—including two who held the summit appointment of Prefect of Egypt, at a time when the total number of pro-curatorships numbered barely fifty.[1] In his seventh satire Juvenal devotes some space to a sneer at Roman knights from the Asiatic provinces: ' I cannot swear in court that I have seen what I have not seen, like a knight of Asia or Bithynia, Cappadocia or Galatia '.[2]

I will not delve into the debated question whether Juvenal is to be identified with the like-named equestrian officer of a well-known inscription who secured no promotion.[3] It remains true that the imperial service was the great goal of ambitious men of the Roman middle classes, educated in the schools of rhetoric, and helped on by senatorial patrons who recommended them to the imperial service as much for scholastic as for practical abilities. The process can be

[1] Ti. Claudius Balbillus, pen friend of Claudius, librarian, and Prefect of Egypt in A.D. 55 is the exemplar. Cf. Syme, *Tacitus*, i.508–9. Pflaum, *Les procurateurs équestres*, 173–4. Sherwin-White, *Roman Citizenship*, 190 n. 4. For preliminary experiments earlier, involving men of letters, see Bowersock, *Augustus and the Greeks*, 31 f.

[2] Juvenal, *Sat.* 7.13–16.

[3] *I.L.S.* 2926. Cf. G. Highett, *Juvenal the Satirist* (Oxford, 1954), 32 f.

followed in Pliny's numerous letters of recommendation,[1] and it is delineated in a remarkable passage of Tacitus' *Dialogus* concerning the rise of two famous leading advocates.[2] They lacked, says Tacitus, the recommendation of wealth, birth or even good character. But they ended up as consular senators and *amici principis*, becoming the éminences grises of Vespasian's principate. Few could hope for so much. But given patronage there remained the lesser but solid rewards of the equestrian career. ' Given patronage.' That is the essential condition. The arena of patronage was the Roman society described by Juvenal and Lucian. At every turn the Italian found himself outfaced by the clever *Graeculus*. The proportion of men of eastern Greek origin in the procuratorial service rises steadily throughout the second century.[3] Lucian himself made the grade.[4] The bitterness of this struggle could not find expression in the set debates of the Senate and the historians, because this was a sphere entirely under the control of the emperor, and still regarded conventionally as part of the *domus Caesaris* even in the pages of Tacitus.[5] There was no organized associations of the persons concerned, who were but a tiny proportion of the numerous equestrian class, numbering many thousands, the vast majority of whom took no part in the public imperial administration. This conflict has remained silent, except for the outbursts of Juvenal and the echoes in Lucian. But the remarks of Tacitus in the *Dialogus* are suggestive. Had Eprius Marcellus added oriental origin to his other dis-

[1] E.g. *Epp.* 2.13, 3.2, and 3.8, all concern the promotion of *studiosi* to military posts.
[2] Tac. *Dial.* 8.1–3.
[3] Pflaum, *op. cit.* 193.
[4] Above, p. 70.
[5] E.g. *Hist.* 1.11.1, *Ann.* 4.15.2, 13.1.3, compared with 12.6.6.

qualifications, what an outburst there might have been. For Tacitus shared the prejudice against *Graeculi*. This comes out in a passage of the *Histories* describing the armed forces of Pontus. These had been taken over from a recently abolished kingdom: ' they were given Roman citizenship and rearmed in our fashion, but retained the *licentia* and *desidia*— the indiscipline and idleness—of Greeks '.[1] This is strong language. The worst that Tacitus could find to say about the hated Piso for example, was that he permitted his troops ' desidiam in castris, licentiam in urbibus '.[2]

The anti-Greek prejudice plays a part also in Tacitus' account of the corruption of Nero, who chose to indulge in the least reputable of the Hellenic graces, acting, singing, and racing. Tacitus ushers in this theme with a vast literary shudder: 'vetus illi cupido erat curriculo quadrigarum insistere, nec minus foedum studium cithara ludicrum in modum canere '.[3] These passions were felt to be the worse for being Greek. So Nero tried to explain them away by maintaining that Apollo the Musician was an accepted Roman deity: ' non modo Graecis in urbibus sed Romana apud templa '.[4] Tacitus did not share Pliny's enthusiasm for the more respectable Greek profession of philosophy. First comes the odd statement in the *Agricola* that his hero as a young man pursued philosophy ' beyond what is allowed to a Roman senator '.[5] In his later books Tacitus' attitude is ever ambiguous or neutral. When he is concerned with Roman politicians who had philosophical leanings, he never

[1] *Hist.* 3.47.2.
[2] *Ann.* 2.55.5.
[3] *Ann.* 14.14.1. ' He had long nourished the desire to drive a racing chariot and an equally disgusting passion for singing at a theatrical performance.'
[4] *Ibid.* 2. ' Honoured in Greek and Roman shrines alike.'
[5] *Agricola*, 4.4.

commends them for this. The remarkable Musonius Rufus is mocked for exercising his talents at the wrong moment, in the midst of a civil war preaching to insurgents: ' intempestivam sapientiam '.[1] The Stoic politician Helvidius Priscus, a great hero to the circle of Pliny, does not exactly shine in the senatorial scenes recorded in the *Histories*.[2] Tacitus' own undoubted hero in the *Annals*, Thrasea Paetus, is only revealed late in the narrative as a pupil of the philosophers by the hostile remarks of his accuser about the bad ways of Stoics: ' rigidi et tristes ... spernit religiones abrogat leges ', etc.[3] So too Tacitus decidedly plays down the philosophical interests of Seneca.[4]

Here one remembers the expulsion of the philosophers from Rome by the Flavian regime.[5] Although this arose out of a political quarrel between the emperors and a senatorial clique, it also involved the whole body of esurient Greek professors of philosophy at Rome. Such men as Euphrates, Artemidorus, and the better-known Dio of Prusa were driven out of Rome. The affair produced an atmosphere favourable to the growth of the anti-Graeculus sentiment. It is likely that many serious-minded men of the administrative classes sympathized with the policy of the regime. An excerpt from Cassius Dio preserves a report of the advice supposedly given to Vespasian by his minister Licinius Mucianus.[6] It contains an attack on the Stoics in the tradition

[1] *Hist.* 3.81.1.

[2] *Ibid.* 4.9, 43.

[3] *Ann.* 16.22.3, 6. ' Stiff and gloomy ... despising the cult of the gods and setting aside legal usages.'

[4] In the long descriptions of the interview between Nero and Seneca and of Seneca's suicide (*Ann.* 14.52–6, 15.61–4) there are only brief references to Seneca's philosophical interests. *Ann.* 14.53.5, 56.4, 6, and 15.62.2.

[5] This has been much discussed. Cf. C. Wirszubski, *Libertas as a political idea at Rome* (Cambridge, 1950), 143 ff.

[6] Dio 65(66).13.1a.

of Juvenal: 'they are full of empty boasting, and if one of
them lets his beard grow long and wears a coarse cloak . . .
he straightway lays claim to wisdom, courage and righteous-
ness. . . . They look down on everyone and call men of good
family softies, the low-born mean-minded, the handsome
licentious, the wealthy avaricious, and the poor servile.' The
author is countering the strictures of a Lucian; and the
passage speaks for the intense irritation that the Greek
intellectuals could stir up in Roman men of affairs.

Xenophobia recurs in an area of social relationships that
can be connected with the *Graeculus* theme, in the attitude
of the upper classes towards their slaves and freedmen. In
general the Romans have a good reputation by the standards
of antiquity for their treatment of household slaves, and their
generous policy of manumission. An increasing benevolence
appears in the writers and administrators of the Principate,
summed up in the legal principle of *favor libertatis*. But there
is another aspect. From time to time the most humane of
men show a very different attitude when society has been
shocked and frightened by the most feared of crimes, the
murder of a master by a household slave. Tacitus in the
*Annals* records the speech of the great lawyer Cassius
Longinus, justifying the extreme severity of the punishment
exacted by the law: the execution of the whole servile staff
resident in the house of the murdered master at that time.[1]
His argument is that slaves, in the great numbers that were
employed in the palaces of Roman magnates, were untrustworthy because of their alien race and culture; he contrasts
the foreign slave with the faithful house-born *verna*. ' Post-
quam . . . nationes in familiis habemus quibus diversi ritus,
externa sacra aut nulla sunt, conluviem istam non nisi metu

[1] *Ann.* 14.43–4.

coercueris.' ' You can only control the foreign scum by fear '.[1] Such is the principle of Longinus. He may have been a severe and inhuman legalist, but the kindly Pliny, famous for his humanitarian attitude towards his servants, betrays exactly the same reaction as Longinus when he relates the murder of Larcius Macedo.[2] This man had been a master of exceptional brutality. It was no great surprise when his slaves attacked him in his bath and flung him on to the furnace to finish him off. The household was duly punished, and Pliny, like Cassius, approved. He ends the account with an interestingly irrational outburst. ' See what dangers and insults we are exposed to. You cannot hope to secure your safety by kindliness and indulgence. They murder us indiscriminately, out of sheer criminality.'[3] But that is quite contrary to the facts about Macedo that Pliny reported half a page earlier. Pliny like Cassius reveals the panic of the wealthy slave-owner isolated amid alien hordes.

A similar tone can be detected in the hysterical attitude that Pliny and Tacitus both adopt towards the memory, rather than the living fact, of the influence enjoyed by the Greek freedmen of the imperial secretariat and household in the time of Claudius and Nero. Pliny, discovering the epitaph of Antonius Pallas, the financial secretary of Claudius, was moved to vast indignation at the thought of the honours voted to the imperial freedman by the Roman senate. He pours his indignation out in one of the longest of all his letters.[4] Pliny's bitterness derives from the fact that the honours were given to an ex-slave. He ignores the mitigating fact that Pallas was a freedman of long standing, calls him a slave throughout, and heaps abuse on him.[5] He stresses the

[1] *Ibid.* 44.5.     [2] Pliny, *Epp.* 3.14.     [3] *Ibid.* 5.
[4] *Ibid.* 8.6.     [5] *Ibid.* 14, cf. *ibid.* 7.29.3.

insolence of a slave coolly declining civic honours offered by the Roman senate. Tacitus picks upon the same instance, and satirically adds that Pallas claimed to be descended from Arcadian kings.[1] Elsewhere Tacitus regularly harps on the excessive influence of imperial freedmen, and the unusual honours that they received, notably the grant of the golden rings, otherwise reserved for Roman knights of impeccable ancestry.[2] The bitterness of tone is the more remarkable in that the honours were largely illusory and formal. The emperor Claudius did not turn his freedmen into senators or knights by the grant of the golden rings or the right to wear the *ornamenta* of a praetor.[3] Besides, in the time of Pliny and Tacitus the imperial freedmen had lost their former prominence. Domitian, Trajan and Hadrian eliminated freedmen from most of the headships of secretariats, and no freedman since the death of Nero had enjoyed anything like the private influence of a Pallas or a Polyclitus over his emperor. The attitude of Tacitus and Pliny is very different from that of Petronius in the *Cena*, who laughs good-temperedly at the vulgarities of the wealthy freedman Trimalchio. The difference may lie in a certain narrowing of the gap between the freedman class and the senatorial aristocracy. Pliny like his uncle Secundus, Tacitus like his father-in-law Agricola, were senators of provincial origin, or from the remote borderland of north Italy. They were of the class that the senators of Claudius' day disliked as newcomers and aliens.[4] And there were even senators whose free origins were in doubt. Tacitus

---

[1] Tac. *Ann.* 12.53.3.

[2] *Ann.* 12.1–2, 60.6, 13.14.1–2, 14.39.1–2. *Hist.* 1.13.1, 2.57.2, 3.12.3, 4.39.1.

[3] Pliny, *Epp.* 8.6.4, cf. 7.29.3 ' hoc coenum . . . ille furcifer '.

[4] Tac. *Ann.* 11.23.4–5.

asserts this as a general fact, without instances.[1] Modern investigations have failed to track down any large number of such senators of servile ancestry. But the intrusion of a single instance sufficed. Such a one was Larcius Macedo, a praetorian senator of whom Pliny gravely remarked, ' servisse patrem suum parum ... meminisset '.[2] Precisely because they were conscious of their own lack of noble birth, men like Pliny were all the more hostile to any who had risen from yet lower down the social scale. So once again it is in the environment of a very narrow society which felt itself threatened by alien elements that xenophobia makes itself felt.

## Antisemitism in the Roman World

The Roman governing class, an imperial people enjoying unfettered power and immense wealth, could afford to show an extreme tolerance to the ways of foreign people who were in no position to challenge their privileges. That tolerance is modified only by restricted and occasional displays of prejudice towards Celts and *Graeculi*. But in one area of the Roman empire racial prejudice manifested itself at full strength. This was between the Greeks and Jews inhabiting the Greek cities of the eastern provinces that had acquired large Jewish colonies in the Hellenistic period. The relationship between Greeks and Jews is well documented in the histories of Josephus, in two tracts of Philo, and in certain documents from Roman Egypt. The feeling was reciprocal. Greek disliked Jew, and Jew disliked Greek.[3] Certain Greek

[1] *Ibid.* 13.27.2.

[2] Pliny, *Epp.* 3.14.1. ' He too often forgot that his own father had been a slave.'

[3] Discussion of the technical position of Judaism in the Roman empire as a tolerated sect, mostly in the context of the Christian persecutions, has overshadowed the question of antisemitism (cf. e.g. S. L. Guterman, *Religious*

writers, followed in due course by the Latins, explain clearly the reasons for this dislike. Its roots lay in the refusal of the Jewish communities to come to terms with the Hellenistic civilization, by their social aloofness from the life of the Greek cities in which they lived. Diodorus, writing under Augustus, stresses the difference of social and religious custom and sums it up in strong terms: ' lack of human feeling '—ἀπανθρωπία —' dislike of strangers '—μισόξενος—and ' hostility towards the human race '—τὸ μῖσος τὸ πρὸς τοὺς ἀνθρώπους.[1] A century later Josephus quotes the Greek Apion for the view that ' the Jews have no goodwill towards the people of another race ', an opinion that he seeks to mollify in a few passages of his histories.[2] All this amounts to one form of modern racial bias: ' *They* won't have anything to do with *us*.' The implication is that the Greeks were willing to accept the other side, but the Jewish people were positively hostile to alien contacts. This is a situation that does not normally occur in the assimilative Graeco-Roman world. It occurs here with great force because Greeks and Jews were mixed up together on a large scale in the cities of Syria and Asia Minor.

But first there is a Greek witness who writes about the Jews

*Toleration and Persecution in ancient Rome* (London, 1951), which has been mainly treated in connection with the riots at Alexandria (below p. 92, n. 1), or with events of the later Empire (cf. J. Vogt, *Kaiser Julian und das Judentum* (Morgenland, H.30). M. Radin, *The Jews among the Greeks and Romans* (Philadelphia, 1915), surveys Hellenistic antisemitism and its terminology (*ibid.* 163 f., 176 ff., 191 ff.). We are not here concerned with the great rebellions.

[1] Diodorus emphasizes this twice—first in his account of Antiochus Epiphanes (34.fr.1.1–4) and then in a general account of Judaea at the time of the Roman conquest (40.fr.3.4).

[2] Jos. *c. Apionem* 2.11. Elsewhere in his two vast books Josephus only twice admits and tries to palliate the charge, once in an account of Solomon in *Ant.* 8.4.3, and once obscurely in *Bell. Jud.* 2.17.3. Here one notes the characteristic phenomenon of the subject of race prejudice showing an insufficient awareness of the traits that cause him to be disliked.

without any of these prejudices. I mean Strabo, in his account of the Jewish religion.[1] This he explains in Greek terms as a kind of pure monotheism superior in its original form to Greek and Egyptian anthropomorphic beliefs and idolatry, but spoiled later by the introduction of superstitious practices, such as food taboos and circumcision. He then adds that the Jews were a civilized people, πολιτικοί, whose social system drew its authority, like that of all civilized peoples, from a basic ordinance, a πρόσταγμα κοινόν, which in their case was of divine origin. He compares Moses, as the intermediary of this authority, to the Spartan Lycurgus, and other such figures. Strabo says nothing about ἀπανθρωπία or separatism, and nowhere in his book discusses the Jews outside Judaea. Yet he himself came from one of the great cities of Asia Minor, among which we find plenty of evidence for an active persecution of Jewish settlers, not merely by their irritated neighbours but by the civic governments.

This emerges very clearly from the remarkable collection of official Roman documents and city decrees published by Josephus in Book XIV (ch. 10) of his *Antiquities*. Their total effect is given by a later passage which describes the situation in Cyrenaica in the time of Augustus:[2] ' Now the cities ill-treated the Jews in Asia and those who lived in Libya and adjacent Cyrene. The former kings had given them equal privileges with the Greeks, but the Greeks affronted them at this time, and that so far as to confiscate their sacred money

---

[1] Strabo 16.2.35–8 (760–62). Cf. the unprejudiced fragment, quoted by Josephus *Ant.* 14.7.2 on Jews in Alexandria. For Strabo's source see W. Aly, *op. cit.* (above p. 2, n. 1) 191 ff. If Posidonius is rightly depicted as an antisemite by Jos. *c. Ap.* 2.7, he may be excluded. Note the contrast with Diodorus, though both give a similar theological account of Judaism.

[2] *Ant.* 16, 6, 1. W. Whiston's translation is used, with variations, throughout.

and to do them mischief on other particular occasions. So when the Jews found no end to the barbarian treatment that the Greeks meted out to them, they sent ambassadors to Augustus.' The bulk of the documents that Josephus quotes are earlier than this, coming from the period of the Roman civil wars of 49–32 B.C. In them we find the supreme Roman authorities requiring the Greek cities of Asia to allow the Jewish colonies free exercise of assembly for religious purposes, the right to practice their social-religious customs, the right to settle their internal legal controversies by their own jurisdiction, and also to collect and despatch to Jerusalem annual offerings in money. These privileges represented a considerable diminution of the ordinary powers of the local government over resident foreigners, and were resented. So the Greek city officials had long been trying to suppress all these activities. At Miletus and Parium a specific decree had been passed by the city assemblies to this end. At Sardes the importation of Jewish foodstuffs had been prohibited. At Ephesus Jews had been fined for celebrating the Sabbath. One document remarks that emissaries of Tralles tried to prevent Roman intervention on behalf of the Jews. At Halicarnassus and Ephesus Roman pressure secured the sanction of a fine against any magistrate who prevented the Jewish faithful from keeping the Sabbath.[1] The documents in Josephus all concern the Roman province of Asia. No fewer than eight cities came under Roman pressure for their anti-semitic activities, some of them more than once. There was also a general Roman edict of toleration issued collectively to all the cities of Asia.[2]

[1] *Ant.* 14.10.8, Parium; 21, Miletus; 20, Tralles; 23, Halicarnassus: 24, Sardes; 25, Ephesus.
*Ibid.* 11.

Thus in the late Republican period the Greek cities of Asia showed their dislike of the Jewish settlements by persistent and effective official persecution. This was checked by Roman intervention, but without complete success. Complaints of persecution were made again during the Principate of Augustus, who reaffirmed the privileges of the Jews.[1] The particular complaints on this occasion suggest that persecution in the Greek cities was now much more restricted. The civic officials dared not openly defy the general principle of toleration that the Romans had imposed, but they could concoct ingenious difficulties. One dodge was to summon Jews involved in ordinary litigation to attend at the civic lawcourts on the Sabbath; when they did not appear they forfeited their suit. In Cyrenaica a system had been devised of preventing the Jews from sending their contributions to Jerusalem by charging them with failure to pay their normal provincial taxes. There is also clear evidence of plain hooliganism. Augustus found it necessary to provide severe penalties against those who stole sacred books and monies from the synagogues. Evidently the civic magistrates were apt to turn a blind eye to such offences.

We may suppose that these measures of Augustus were fairly effective, though their enforcement would still depend on the local courts rather than the Roman governors. Josephus found no more documents to quote for half a century. Then, as is well known, the emperor Claudius had to deal with difficulties that had arisen in Judaea itself, at Egyptian Alexandria and even at Rome, as a result of the folly of the emperor Gaius in trying to impose the imperial cult upon the Jews. Claudius in addition saw fit to reaffirm the general privileges of the Jewish settlements everywhere.[2]

[1] *Ant.* 16.6.2, 4, 5.   [2] *Ibid.* 19, 5.3.

This decree is couched in universal terms; it refers to no
specific abuses, and quotes the decree of Augustus as the last
enactment dealing with the matter. It would seem that the
Greek populations had exploited the opportunity provided
by the Roman civil wars to oppress their Jewish residents.
Then the restoration of effective Roman authority checked
the worst of these excesses, though the basic situation remained
unchanged.

The great rebellion in Judaea itself in Nero's last years set
off an astonishing outburst of antisemitic violence in Greek
cities of adjacent areas. This was of a kind and on a scale that
had never taken place before. It began with the expulsion and
partial massacre of the whole Jewish population of the Greek
city of Caesarea, the seat of the Roman governor of Judaea.[1]
Jewish reprisals followed in areas of mixed population like
the Decapolis. All this may be regarded as part and parcel of
the Judaean revolt. But the example spread further afield.
Josephus records the organized massacre of ten thousand
persons at Damascus, and the pattern spread to northern
Syria.[2] He states that only Antioch and Apamea in the north,
and Sidon in the south, were immune from such massacres.[3]
'The disorders in all Syria were terrible,' he writes, ' every
city was divided into two armies that were encamped against
each other.'[4] But more revealing is his account of events at
Antioch, where a large Jewish colony lived under the
authority of the Greek city and the eye of the Roman provincial governor.[5] The story is rather confused. First it
seems a rumour was spread of a plot by the Jews to burn the
city down. This led to the execution of suspected persons and
to the unauthorized suppression of the Jewish communal

[1] *Bell. Jud.* 2.18, 1.    [2] *Ibid.* 2.20.2.    [3] *Ibid.* 2.18.5.
[4] *Ibid.* 2.18.2.    [5] *Ibid.* 7.3.3–4.

privileges. Then an actual fire destroyed many public buildings. Only the presence of a Roman official prevented riots
and massacres. Finally, when the revolt in Judaea was óver,
the people of Antioch petitioned Titus, the Roman supreme
commander, when he visited the city, to expel the whole
Jewish population.[1] When he refused, they requested the
abolition of all the former communal privileges of the Jews
at Antioch. This too Titus refused.

There is no record of any trouble outside Syria at this time.
The violence is untypical of the Empire, and the large po-
groms were limited to the borderlands of Judaea. But the
suspicious and unfriendly relationship revealed by the story
of Antioch is akin to the situation in Asia a century earlier,
and to that which prevailed at Egyptian Alexandria throughout the first and second century A.D. For the Graeco-Judaic
troubles at Alexandria there is full documentation of affrays
and petitions to Rome in the time of Claudius, who in a long
letter addressed to the city tried to calm all parties and to
prevent either from damaging the other. The anti-semitic
feeling also appears in the curious compositions known as the
' Acts of the Pagan Martyrs', though it is not their sole
concern. As much has been written about these affairs in
recent years I shall not dilate upon this part of the evidence.[2]
The situation is much as in the cities of Asia and Syria,
exacerbated by the great size of the Jewish community at
Alexandria, and the belief that the Jews enjoyed more official

[1] *Ibid.* 7.5.2.
[2] See E. M. Smallwood, *Philonis legatio ad Gaium* (Leiden, 1961), 3 ff.
H. I. Bell, ' Antisemitism in Alexandria ', *J.R.S.* 1941, 1 ff. H. A. Musurillo,
*The Acts of the Pagan Martyrs* (Oxford, 1954), 256–8. M. Radin, *op. cit.*
p. 86, n. 3 above. The letter of Claudius (P. Lond. 1912, ll.14–108) is
available in M. P. Charlesworth, *Documents illustrating the reigns of Claudius
and Nero* (Cambridge, 1939) n. 2. Josephus, *Bell. Jud.* 2.18.7, summarizes the
historical position at Alexandria.

favour from Rome than did the somewhat disloyal and anti-Roman Greek population.

In modern times there are two distinct patterns of race-prejudice. The alien element may be disliked simply for its otherness, the dissimilarity of its customs, and its exclusiveness. It may also be feared as a competitor, either economic or political or both. The two patterns may but need not both be present and work together. In the Roman empire the pattern of exclusiveness is dominant. The Jews were disliked because of their refusal to cooperate in the Hellenistic civilization, while coexisting in large groups inside the Greek cities. But it is somewhat surprising that so much happens if there was no element of competition at all. The sources are entirely silent about economic rivalry of any sort. Equally, by their very exclusiveness the resident Jewish aliens in Greek cities were not able to compete for political power and office at the expense of the Greeks. Their desire was to live a closed communal life under the authority of their local ethnarchs. But there is an obscure exception to this. It is well documented that at Alexandria the Jewish residents tried to infiltrate into the local Greek citizenship, to which they were not entitled.[1] At Syrian Antioch Josephus records something similar. Antiochus Epiphanes, he says, had granted the Jews ' a habitation at Antioch and . . . the enjoyment of equal rights with the Greeks themselves '.[2] These were the privileges, still in force under Roman rule, that Titus refused to cancel. Nothing of this sort is documented for the cities of Asia, but at the small south Syrian city of Dora the Jews

---

[1] The controversy over the status of the Jews at Alexandria seems to be resolved by the letter of Claudius, which shows that Josephus' representation of them as full citizens of the Greek city is false, despite A. Momigliano, *Claudius the Emperor and his Achievement*, 96 n. 25.

[2] *Bell. Jud.* 7.3.3.

tried to interpret the decree of Claudius about their communal privileges to mean that they enjoyed equal rights with the Greek citizens.[1] So too in the cities of Cyrenaica Josephus claimed that ' the former kings had given them equal rights '.[2] Even if through your religion you were unable to take part in the political life of a Greek city, the local franchise afforded advantages in the relationships of private life. It would seem that Jewish communities outside Judaea were trying to have it both ways: to live as self-contained Judaic colonies, and at the same time to secure the private advantage of local citizenship, while refusing to share in the burdens and duties of local government. The Greek element, equally devoted to the principle of local autonomy and to the control of their own cities, disliked these enclaves. It was not surprising if animosity intensified in such circumstances. The emperor Claudius in his letter to Alexandria remarked sharply: 'I bid the Jews to stop trying to secure more than they had before. Let them be satisfied with their own proper position . . . and make the most of their abundant advantages in what is not their own city.' [3]

Where there was no effective control over the local government, the Jewish community could fare very ill. This appears from events within the Parthian empire about A.D. 39–40. The Jews at Babylon and Seleucia, Hellenized cities of Mesopotamia which the Parthians largely left to themselves, fell into trouble by asserting themselves against the local governments.[4] At Babylon Josephus says: ' The Jews were almost always at variance with the Babylonians by

---

[1] *Ant.* 19.6.3—in Josephus' version of the letter of Petronius to Dora.

[2] *Ant.* 16.6.1. Cf. similar claims at Caesarea, *Bell. Jud.* 2.13.7, 14.4.

[3] P. Lond. *ad fin.*

[4] *Ant.* 18.9.8–9.

reason of the diversity of their laws, and whichever party grew boldest assaulted the other.' Driven out of Babylon, the colony moved to Seleucia, a great city where the Greeks were at loggerheads with the unprivileged native population, which Josephus called ' Syrian '. He relates how the Jews sided with the Syrians against the Greeks, thus giving the Syrians the upper hand. But Greeks and Syrians patched up their quarrel, and both turned on the Jewish immigrants. There was a great massacre, and the remnant fled to northern Mesopotamia.

There was another factor also at work. Josephus remarks that at Antioch, ' the Jews made converts of a great number of the Greeks perpetually, and thus after a sort brought them to be a portion of their own body '.[1] So too at Damascus: ' Yet did the Damascenes distrust their wives, which were almost all addicted to the Jewish religion.'[2] Nothing prevented a Hellene from becoming an adherent of Judaism of the class known as ' the Pious '—a sort of half-Jew—while remaining an active Hellene in his city. But it did not work the other way round. Phil-hellene Jews existed who toyed with cultural Hellenism, but they still claimed the separatist privileges of their religion. These included in two great cities, Antioch and Alexandria, the possession of a special quarter of the city to live in.[3] Josephus regards this as a great advantage; it was not a sign of inferior or repressed status. There was nothing of the mediaeval ghetto about these quarters. But their existence emphasized the separatism of the Jewish community within the very cities where they tried to infiltrate into the local franchise. Prejudice arising from this separatism continued to ferment between Greeks and Jews.

[1] *Bell Jud.* 7.3.3.    [2] *Ibid.* 2.20.2.
[3] *Ibid.* 2.18.8, 7.3.3. *Ant.* 14.7.2.

It was intensified by the success with which under Roman protection the Jewish colonies maintained their isolation, while at the same time penetrating the enemy's position by religious proselytism on a large scale.

I have been talking so far about the Greek attitude. What of the Romans? The Roman administration has appeared so far as the consistent champion of Jewish privileges. And so it continued. Despite two scaring rebellions in Judaea, under Nero and Hadrian, and a third in the time of Trajan that devastated the Greek provinces of Cyprus and Cyrenaica, and parts of Egypt, it is remarkable how the Roman government maintained its policy of protecting the privileges of the Diaspora. So too at Rome itself, where a large resident population existed, that tended to be involved in riots for reasons that remain wholly obscure. The emperors Tiberius and Claudius each once lost his temper and expelled large numbers of Jews.[1] But they soon returned, and this local irritation did not alter the general philo-Judaic attitude of the government. Claudius in his letter to Alexandria, though suspicious of some aspects of Jewish activity, yet strove to be scrupulously fair to both parties, Hellenes and Jews alike.

Despite the follies of Gaius, the Jews frequently had friends in high places. The influence of King Agrippa with Claudius, of the convert Poppaea with Nero, and of the beautiful Berenice with Titus, are well known. The so-called ' Acts of the Pagan Martyrs ' give from the view-point of upper-class Greeks of Alexandria a semi-historical version of their struggle with the Jewish community in a series of trials before the tribunal of the emperors. They are consistent in regarding the Roman emperors as philo-Judaean. Nowhere is this more remarkable than in the ' Acts of Hermaiscus '.

[1] Tac. *Ann.* 2.85.5. Suet. *Claudius* 25.3. Dio 57.18.5a, 60.6.6.

The empress Plotina is there depicted as the protectress of Jewish interests, and the Alexandrian representative accuses Trajan of having his imperial cabinet packed with ' profane Jews '—ἀνόσιοι Ἰουδαῖοι.[1]

What of private and unofficial opinion at Rome? There is remarkably little evidence. Tacitus gives an account of Jewish customs and religion in the *Histories*.[2] He did not care for them, and takes much the same line as the hostile Greek tradition. He embitters the usual charges of separatism with particular slanders, and stresses the objectionable behaviour, from the Roman viewpoint, of converts who ' abandon their gods and cast aside their own country '. He gives a summary of the Jewish religion that is akin to Strabo's account, but without any of his approval. Tacitus seems to approve of nothing that he mentions about the Jews, except, grudgingly, their progenitivity. He does not even approve them for refusing to worship rulers and emperors. Finally he remarks, contrasting their cult practices with Graeco-Roman ritual: ' Iudaeorum mos absurdus sordidusque '. ' Their usage is pointless and mean.' The elder Pliny also, like Tacitus, did not care for Jews. He gives no general description, yet manages to release two barbed shafts against them, as a people that ' savages its own vitals ', and is ' famous for its contempt of the gods '.[3]

Juvenal is more explicit. He was acquainted with the Jewish community at Rome, and has more extensive though less accurate information about their usages than Tacitus. In his *Satire on Women* Judaism appears among the cults

[1] Musurillo, *op. cit.* 44–45, n. viii, 25 f., 42 f.

[2] Tac. *Hist.* 5.5. A. M. A. Hospers-Jansen, *Tacitus over de Joden* (Groningen, 1949), with an English summary, is mainly concerned with the source question.

[3] Pliny, *Nat. Hist.* 12.113, 13.46.

favoured by wealthy ladies. He describes how 'in secret session a Jewess with trembling limbs, the high missionary of the laws of Jerusalem, mutters like a beggar into a lady's ear'. The lady rewards her sparingly. 'The Jews sell you any dream you want for small change.' [1] Juvenal, like the elder Pliny, classes the Jews among professors of magic and prophesy. [2] In his third satire he speaks incidentally of the Jewish quarter at Rome by the shrine of Egeria: 'The sacred buildings are now all let out to Jewish beggars with their baskets and bundles of hay.' [3] At greater length in Satire 14, on parents and children, there is a sketch of a Roman convert's son, whom he calls a sky-worshipper. [4] The man refuses to eat pork and remains idle every seventh day. In a most hostile tone Juvenal brings in the theme of anti-social separatism: 'Romanas soliti contemnere leges, Iudaicum ediscunt et servant . . . ius.' [5] This usage he characterizes as 'refusing to show the way to a traveller or to give him a drink of water unless he is a fellow-worshipper'. The effect is much the same as in Tacitus, though the emphasis is different. Juvenal reveals dislike, but no violent animus. There is an overall impression of poverty and meanness, that recalls the final gibe of Tacitus—*mos sordidus*—and suggests that a large part of the Jewish colony at Rome was by no means wealthy.

If Juvenal's Jewish sketches are compared with his *Graeculus esuriens*, a notable difference emerges. Juvenal may dislike the alien ways of the Jews, but he does not fear them as competitors in any way. In a Rome full of aliens and alien sects the Jewish colony was only one among many. Though

---

[1] Juv. *Sat.* 6.541–7.    [2] Pliny, *Nat. Hist.* 30.11.
[3] Juv. *Sat.* 3.13–16.    [4] *Ibid.* 14.96–106.
[5] 'It is their way to despise the laws of Rome while studying to learn and keep the rules of Jewry.'

Jews could and did become Roman citizens, their religion made it impossible for them to take any part in the lucrative professions or the public employments of the imperial service. The principal path to promotion for men of all classes, the Roman army, was barred to Jews of all classes as a favour of their own seeking. Roman citizens of Jewish origin were exempted from military service from the time of Julius Caesar onwards.[1] It seems from the sneers of Juvenal that the Jewish colony at Rome was somewhat proletarian in composition. Unlike the magnates of the western provinces and the ambitious Greeks of the east, Jews of good family did not try to mount the ladder that led to procuratorships and seats in the Roman senate. The great exception, the well-known Julius Alexander, who ended his equestrian career as prefect of Egypt in A.D. 68, was a renegade from his faith.[2] So the relationship between native citizens and alien Jews at Rome itself was much more relaxed than in the Greek cities of the east, despite the presence of a large Jewish colony and the occasional riots and expulsions.

You may call the attitude of Juvenal and Tacitus anti-semitic, because it is a dislike of Jews based on their way of life. But it is a negative anti-semitism. No violent action followed from it, if only because the Jews were knocking on no Roman doors.

I have called this antagonism racial for convenience. But this is misleading. Though Greeks and Latins refer to the Jews as an ἔθνος or a *natio* or a *gens*, i.e. a folk or tribe, there is no genuinely racial or racist connotation. The distinction is political, social and religious, national rather than genetic. The large mass of converts among other peoples prevented the racial idea from developing. Besides, the Jews of Judaea would

---

[1] Jos. *Ant.* 14.10.14, 16, 18.  [2] *Ibid.* 20.5.2.

not differ physically from other Aramaic or Greek-speaking inhabitants of the Levant.

There remains the question of the discouragement of Jewish religious proselytism and the prosecution of Romans for practising Judaism. This is an ill-documented business. It concerned only Roman citizens of non-Jewish origin who adopted Judaism. Large numbers of Jewish nationals became Roman citizens with full recognition of their special status: they were not expected to drop their native religion on becoming Roman citizens.[1] Judaism as an external sect was treated no differently from other alien cults which persons who were Roman citizens by birth were, nominally, not supposed to practice. There was no special discrimination against Judaism. The occasional enforcement of the nominal veto was directed against persons of high society for political reasons that had nothing to do with religious or racial prejudice. Juvenal shows clearly in the passage about the son of a proselyte that for the great mass of the population of Rome the nominal ban was a dead letter. Even Hadrian's specific veto on circumcision was of limited intention; it was not part of a general veto on proselytism or Jewish practices.[2]

The overall picture is plain. In Greek and Roman society of the empire period there was some dislike of the Jewish communities based on their separatism and alienation, although Judaism as a religion was gaining much ground in the very same quarters. Only in Greek cities where a large Jewish colony existed, that asserted itself politically against the interests of the Greek majority, was their presence felt as a menace that required repression or violent counter-action.

[1] p. 99, n. 1 above.
[2] Dio 67.14.1–3, 68.1.2. *Digest* 48.8.4.2, 11 pr. *Sent. Pauli* V.22.3–4. See my *Roman Society and Roman Law in the New Testament* (Oxford, 1963), 81 n. 2; E. M. Smallwood, *Cl. Phil.* (1956), 1 ff. and *Latomus* 20 (1961), 93 ff.

At Rome there is a certain analogy between the regard for Judaism and that for Hellenism. Both spread, and both could be disliked. Despite, or because of, the cultural supremacy of Hellenism, there was a reaction against the usages of the resident *Graeculus*. Because he was a professional rival in upper-class society, he stirred up more active resentment than did Judaeus Apelles. Back at the beginnings of the period Cicero with impartial invective stirred up the prejudices of his equestrian jurymen, in his defence of the dubious Flaccus, equally against the lying levity of the witnesses from Asiatic Hellas, and against the alien and barbarous superstition of the Jewish colonies.[1]

Standing back from all this what does one conclude? The raw material and the basic attitudes of racial and cultural prejudice existed in the upper-class society of the late republic and of the Principate. There were well-known techniques for exploiting such emotions if occasion demanded it, and it would seem that potentially the market, or the favourable audience, was large, large enough to determine an issue in the Roman senate, or before a numerous jury in the political courts at Rome. But ' occasional ' and ' potential ' are the key words. Both from Strabo and from Caesar it emerges clearly that as between Romans and northern barbarians, the essential factor of fear was lacking. They might dislike certain traits of barbarians, and still more of savages, but conscious superiority in the techniques of civilization and warfare negatived the potential forces that might have worked up steam in different circumstances. The contrast with the bitter rivalry—under certain conditions—of Romans with the *Graeculus esuriens*, and of Greeks with Jewish immigrants, all people of recognized culture, is instructive.

[1] Cicero, *pro Flacco* 53–66, 66–69.

# INDEX

# Index

# Index

# Index

# Index

# INDEX OF GREEK WORDS